In Times of Transition

ISBN: 978-1-910181-80-5

Printed and Published in Great Britain by
BookPrintingOnline part or AnchorPrint Group Ltd 2020

Published: September 2020

In Times of Transition

Dedicated to the memory of Pauline, whom
I loved,
and to whom I owe so much

Pauline and David holding the 2012 Olympic Torch
during the Nottingham lap of its relay

Contents

Photographs

Introduction

In our times of transition
There is a change of ambition
To accept what is good.

In later times of transition
We change from much doing
To being.

In times of transition
We need good friendships
As colleagues to travel on the way.

At the end of transition
May we change -
To fullness of life.

Reaching towards eternity
And the perfect love of God.

Life is about exploration with many stages on the journey. We never stop learning. For most of my journey I have been an Ordained Methodist Church presbyter - simply called ministers. In more recent times my blog has provided me with an opportunity to send out a monthly letter to friends and pastoral contacts made.

It is in response to the requests of several friends that I present these letters as an anthology. My hope is that readers will find thoughts amongst these writings that will relate to their own situation whatever life-stage they have reached.

Each year's collection is prefaced by thoughts and experiences relating to that period. The letters touch on trends in daily life, changing situations in the world and life in the city of Nottingham. They do not follow any progressive theme and, for this reason, do need reading slowly and individually, but they do try to show facets of every-day living. Many issues are not touched upon-mainly because they are already being considered in newspapers, radio and TV. This is not because these issues are to be ignored. Caring about the natural world, the misuse of nuclear power, totalitarian dictatorships, the sin of racism, gender issues, criminality, greed, exclusiveness, and many other issues do affect our future. Let no older person say, 'I may no longer be around when undesirable things happen', but encourage other generations to see the value of good neighbourliness and ecology whether local or world-wide in their own lifetime.

Over the last 60 years there have been tremendous changes in our culture, outlook and likewise in ministry. The older we are the more likely we are to have been influenced by our earlier outlooks. There is a greater temptation to reminisce.

The monthly letter is read in many different situations. This came out strongly in a review made in October 2017 where the readership content turned out to be friends of recent and long-standing, people in leadership roles, in policing, church life, education, health and care homes, and those who join in an informal prayer time, wherever they are, in what is called 'Prayers at 12.' The readership now includes many more friends living on their own, and others whose background is unknown.'

Social media used by those who stir up strife and hatred in the world or satisfy narcissistic tendencies can cause great harm, but the media are also a tremendous force for creating a sense of community, cohesion and fellowship for like minds, and 'the common good.'

The letters spring out of devotional themes, reflections based on day-to-day occurrences, chaplaincy work, and experiences of a more personal kind. Some letters have been used by others as short devotional talks, or in church magazines. Earlier letters are set in traditional church pastoral settings. Later they reach out to a wider community. In their original form the letters begin with 'dear friends' or 'dear everyone.' The headings to each letter have been added since. Each issue ends with 'all good wishes', 'every blessing' or just 'sincerely David', but every letter has a personal touch.

The title 'In Times of Transition' has been chosen because these letters, written over the last nine years seek to reflect how someone now in his late eighties finds fresh challenges which require a positive response, and even more so in the Covid-19 pandemic. They also cover themes that have come to mind between the fiftieth year of my Ordination and now - the sixtieth!

Chapter 1: 2010 - 11

Life is full of the unexpected

There is inevitably a slight touch of preaching in these letters. One of the skills of getting a message over is to pick up illustrations from everywhere, relate them to insights in Holy Scripture and interpret them in a way that makes them part of a living message for today. The Biblical prophets certainly picked their illustrations from every aspect of life, and in some instances even turned them into acted oracles. I believe that it is still possible for us even in a very secular age to get good examples of how to live by the observation of every-day happenings. When I began this series of monthly letters, it would not have been possible to know how much grief, and illness successfully treated by surgery, would come along to affect my ways of thinking and my response.

'For everything there is a season,' says the writer of the book of Ecclesiastes, 'A time to be born and a time to die.' From a Christian view point we do believe there is another 'dimension' which we often describe as life-everlasting in Christ, life beyond death. Nevertheless, the loss of a loved one, in spite of our beliefs and hopes of eternal life is frequently very painful. There is, between all the seasons of life, a time of transition. Each stage has its own characteristics, but they do not necessarily come in the same order for everyone.

There has been a great deal of research in recent years into the lives of older people; their lifestyles, health, and approaches to life. There is a need however for older people to express personally their attitudes to life and the experiences that shaped them. This is not a task to leave to research students alone, or well-known personalities who are just on the edge of getting old. There is need especially for 'older' old people to help those who are wondering how life will fare for them. Strange as it may seem, those in the later stages of life, do not always feel really old. Younger people in every age group often assume more deterioration and decline in ability amongst those older than themselves than there really is, and might unwittingly be accused of 'ageism'. It is common for many to maintain many of their cognitive skills for the rest of their lives.

It must be added though that there are some pleasant surprises as well as sorrow. When we weigh them up, we see far more blessings than we realised. We can often see things from a different and wider perspective. This was a period in my later seventies when natural physical stamina and cognitive skills were still very much in pristine condition. I had not long completed further studies – not having had the opportunity in earlier life to graduate. This year was a period when there was a sense of fulfilment and pleasant surprises, although still a feeling that many things remained that needed to be done.

October

'Season of mists and mellow fruitfulness'...... and celebration!

Autumn is here with its 'Season of mists and mellow fruitfulness,' writes the poet John Keats'; and 'here' in the northern hemisphere, a time to celebrate the Harvest. It is also a time to remember those whose harvest has been ruined or lost, and to support them wherever we can with our generosity and our prayers.

For some people this season may remind them that they have reached the 'autumn' of their lives. Now, hopefully, they can celebrate a time of mellow fruitfulness and share what they have been given with many of their friends.

This year for us has been a rich time of celebration, our Golden Wedding year, and also the 50th year of my Ordination. They have not always been easy years. I feel the need for the forgiveness of my 'foolish ways,' but above all I do feel a sense of thankfulness for what has been shared together and given to us.

The 'Autumn of The Human Life-Cycle' ideally is meant to be a time of celebration and thankfulness. It is however also a time to give support to others who have not been so fortunate as ourselves. There have been many who have not reached such a landmark who have shared with us in our celebrations.

May God help us at all times to share with others the good things we have received in our lives.

Easter (2011)

Easter is not the end ..., but a New Beginning

Life is full of the unexpected and things rarely work out in the way that we intended! Things turn up 'out of the blue' that worry us: but in contrast, there are occasions when, as CS Lewis put it, we are 'surprised by Joy!'

This was the experience of the first followers of Jesus during Holy Week. There is the jubilation of Palm Sunday, the trial, his agony in the Garden of Gethsemane, the sharing of a Last Supper together with his disciples and the climax of it all, his death on The Cross on Good Friday. It seems to be the end of the story about someone who, on the one hand, was looked upon simply as a 'good man', but recognised by others to be the son of God.

Was this the end of a tragic story?

The women approaching the tomb on the first Easter day were full of gloom and doubt. A sense of doom seemed to be the natural outcome of what had happened, but the message of the angel at the tomb assures them, "He is not here, he is risen!"

The Good News of Easter is this: God works through the unexpected as well as what seems to be the predictable. The message of 'Christ Risen' is to fill us with hope, for in Him, 'Love's redeeming work is done.'

May we all know the Risen Power of Christ in our lives.

A Very Happy Easter!

Pauline too sends her greetings to everyone.

June

'Trust and do not be afraid'

On Pentecost Sunday I took a Church Anniversary service at a small village church but what I didn't know, until six days before, was that it was to be the last Anniversary in their 129-year-old chapel. A great deal of money was needed to repair and keep it warm. Soon they are going to hold their Sunday worship in the village hall.

The congregation was very sad about this change. They felt they were going through a time of great uncertainty; but at least they recognised that a church is more than a building, and needs to adapt itself to changing situations.

I wonder whether we realise however, that the Holy Spirit often does his greatest work through us all when we are going through times of uncertainty?

William Cowper, in one of his hymns, 'God moves in a mysterious way' wrote:

‘Ye fearful saints fresh courage take,

The clouds ye so much dread

Are big with mercy, and shall break

In blessings on your head.’

It is believed to be the last hymn that Cowper wrote. He suffered from depression for most of his life, but when he composed these words, he was saying something very important. He dared to believe that God, through His Spirit, can bring blessings even through difficult times.

This is an aspect of prayer that none of us must overlook. It is all part of what someone recently described as the 'spirituality' of trusting.

May we all learn 'to trust and not be afraid', live out our lives by faith, and see how God frequently is leading us through our dilemmas, worries and challenges.

P.S. On the 28th of this month, I'm due to go to Queen's Medical Centre, Nottingham for Colon cancer surgery. The prognosis is fairly encouraging, but Pauline and I would value your prayers at this time. D.

October

'Don't rush to conclusions...., and always be open...'

Earlier this month I went on a two-day course organised by the National Association of Chaplains to the Police. Fifteen of us from various parts of the country met at Swanwick in the beautiful Derbyshire countryside. We came from cities, market towns and rural areas. We represented

Anglican, Methodist, Baptist, Pentecostalist, House Church and Roman Catholic ministries, and there were two very able course leaders.

Those present included newly appointed chaplains to the police who were there for basic instruction. Others of us had been chaplains for many years.

The course covered a tremendous amount in a very short period, but this in no way detracted from its value.

At the beginning we were asked to 'get to know' the person next to us. We had to do two things: first, we had to say *something about ourselves that was true*, and then, *something that was false*. The person next to me claimed that prior to being a clergyman, he had been 'a teacher of Latin and Greek,' or a 'semi-professional footballer'. Which was true? He taught Latin and Greek.

I said I thought he had been a semi-professional footballer! How deceptive the signals we give off to others can be!

The course, besides being informative on police matters and procedures, was also good in other ways.

Firstly, there was a great sense of fellowship amongst us, simply because we shared a common aim and, in this particular group, a common faith. Fellowship is always at its healthiest when it is turned outward, and not just concerned with itself.

Secondly, there was a sense that we were all learning together. I was by far the oldest person there, but I don't think that mattered. As Christians for example if we have properly understood our faith, we never stop learning. I believe in 'life-long-learning' because all Christians are 'disciples'. The very meaning of the word is 'learners.'

Summing up, it seems to me that the course was saying to me:

Don't rush to conclusions about people.

Enjoy fellowship that is generated by a common aim or purpose, and finally.

May we always be open to learn something new.

(Thanks again for your support in the last three months. I continue to make good progress.)

November

Diwali: Light and Darkness

It was a wet night, and I was feeling my age. I had just been to a lecture at Nottingham University and I was waiting at the campus for a bus into the city.

At the bus stop were about twenty or so Hindu students. They were in an excited mood travelling to Leicester that evening to celebrate Diwali.

The bus was due in about a quarter of an hour and it was really miserable standing at the bus stop in the rain. Then a young Hindu woman student in the party sitting under the sheltered part of the bus stop touched my shoulder and said, “Please take my seat." I thankfully accepted her offer.

This small gesture moved me quite deeply. This group of students were from very different religious background to mine. The incident reminded me of the words of Jesus where he speaks of someone giving a ‘cup of cold water’ to a needy person ‘in his name.’ Perhaps the ‘cold water’ metaphor was not very appropriate on a night like this, but I felt this student was showing a Christ-like act to me.

There was however another aspect of this situation that seemed significant. They were going to celebrate the festival of Diwali, when Hindus remember the victory of light over darkness, of good over evil. To a Christian, their 'festival of light' reminds us of Christ himself who comes as the Light of the World. We shall soon celebrate 'His Coming' once more.

November is a month of remembrance when we recall not only the sacrifices of others in two world wars, but all kinds of other people who have given their lives and have suffered because they have stood on the side of justice and peace.

We thankfully remember them and pray that the forces of light will prevail over darkness. Our prayer must surely be that all faiths will have goodwill in mind when they consider their relationships with people whose outlook and religion are very different from their own. Peace and true prosperity cannot come in the world unless there is a 'helping hand' across people of all outlooks and faiths.

May the peace of Christ be in all our hearts, may we share his peace with others, and may we, too, reach out towards all who are in need.

December

Every human being is unique

This year we have welcomed the seven billionth child into the world. We are beginning to wonder how much longer this phenomenon of human expansion can go on.

Human fertility has halved in recent years. Families are only bringing about half the children into the world that they used to bring in but there is still this colossal increase, and it seems to be the parts of world that can least sustain this tremendous growth where it is happening. The struggle for existence can be exacerbated by this situation. Food can be short, educational opportunities may be very limited for many and there is always the danger of greater racial and ethnic tensions where growth is the greatest.

This is the gloomy side of the picture, but there is also another side. St John's Gospel speaks of the 'light that lightens every man coming into the world.' There is something unique about every human being. There is great joy at the birth of a child in most situations, and all related to this new human being do their best to make the child and this mother comfortable and happy.

There will be the challenge in the days ahead to produce food in a way that is more economical in the use of the world resources and for many people not to be so greedy in what they eat and drink - and the way that they live. Politicians will need to use their skills in a far better way to bring peace and cohesiveness into the world.

Once more we celebrate the coming of the Christ-child. He was born in a situation where there was 'no room'. A very different situation from what we find today but nevertheless even then there were tussles in society as people from different religious and ethnic backgrounds strived to live together.

The cry of the Christmas Carol, 'Joy to the world' has important significance. We have a message of joy in Christ for a crowded world. His task is to bring God and frail human beings together - 'God and sinners reconciled.'

May each one of us share in the task of reconciliation that Christ came into the world to bring about.

May we show goodwill that has a practical and lasting significance towards all our neighbours in the world.

A Happy Christmas - to share with all around us!

Nottingham Christmas Market

Chapter 2: 2012

Coasting along

This was my eightieth year. How much we benefit from good medical care in many parts of the world; but It becomes increasingly important that we live in the best way and with the best sense of purpose that we possibly can. I still believe that there is still much we have to give to others in our older years. It is also true however that every person, whatever their religious or cultural background, needs to keep a sense of purpose. It can be really inspiring to learn from others at this time in our lives what their experience of life has been, as well as to follow good role models ourselves when we are older - just as we did when we were younger. We always need to have a listening ear.

One person I admired greatly as a spiritual leader was Pope John the 23rd who in his eighties brought about a revolution in relationships between Catholics, many Protestants and Christians of all kinds in his whole approach to unity. I also saw him as a role model of what can be achieved in senior years. It must never be assumed that, as we get older, we are to be written off as far as usefulness and purposefulness is concerned, but should simply be accepted for what we are and for what we can still offer.

It was a year when I was still intensely in touch with most things that were going on in the organisational life of the Church as well as pastorally, yet with a greater freedom to live a better-balanced life. There was a strong sense of togetherness between Pauline and myself in so many things that we did. 'Togetherness' is a great source of strength. Although in our case our children are geographically scattered around the country, and actual getting together is not always easy, the bonds stay healthy and good.

Coasting along can have a touch of the humdrum about it; but as John Keble the early 19th-century hymn writer reminds us: 'the trivial round and the common task will furnish all we need to ask.' The humdrum can provide us with the essentials of living a meaningful life because every day happenings, if we are really willing to explore them, provide opportunities to be servants of all, servants of our Creator, and widen our ability to find contentment.

'Walk, talk, think and share.

Be especially aware of opportunities that come along.

Learn to laugh, listen and truly empathise.

"Ordinariness" teaches us how to be wise.'

January

A Minor Miracle?

I thought you might like to hear of something that happened to me just before Christmas.

The Carol Service for the emergency services in Nottinghamshire, is always a major event in the life of the County. It is usually held at Southwell Minster. Members of the fire, ambulance services, and the police take part, with the Lord Lieutenant reading the final lesson. There is the support of some well-known choir, and the rousing music of the Nottinghamshire police band accompanying the singing of carols.

Again, this Christmas, as a police chaplain, I was on parade and, after the service and refreshments, went to the vestry with the other clergy to disrobe. Whilst there the Bishop of Sherwood started to whistle 'Hark the Herald Angels sing.' Without thinking, I joined in whistling with him.

It was the first time I had whistled for 25 years!

A quarter of a century ago whilst in the Shetland Islands, I had an accident with a car garage door. The weighted counterbalance spring broke and hit me in the face, badly cutting my lower lip and damaging my teeth. If the blow had been three inches higher it would have been fatal. For several weeks I was unable to preach, and I lost the ability to whistle altogether.

Now I can whistle again.

A minor miracle?

Life can be full of surprises!

February

On becoming an Octogenarian!

This letter covers a landmark celebration - becoming an Octogenarian! The question I ask myself is this: 'Do I feel any different reaching this age?'

In many ways I don't. I certainly get tired quicker, but my mind still feels tremendously active. I'm extremely thankful for that. I also realise that I am very fortunate to be able to do so much. Taking monthly Holy Communion at a residential care home often reminds me of this, because many there are younger than myself.

Our 'life span' though does have a limited duration, and we should make the best use of our God-given time and the gifts he has given to us.

There is a temptation sometimes when we get older to 'write ourselves off' and feel what we are doing no longer matters to the world, its needs, and the needs of those around us.

We can easily fall into a kind of 'ageism in reverse,' where we take the attitude of saying to ourselves, 'I don't matter'. We have to remember that we always do matter. Every one of us has a 'calling to fulfil'. We always have a role, at the very least, of encouraging and praying for the well-being of all with whom we come into contact, and especially those who do so much for us, and give us their support and help.

John Wesley once said. 'Lord, let me not live to be useless.'

The basic question is this: are we willing for God to decide the ways in which we can be most useful in His world? This is important for the prayer life of us all.

March

Help in low moments

Last month I felt I had 'taken on' more than I could cope with and found myself wondering whether it was all worth it.

A start had to be made with the tasks in hand, and the strange thing was that, immediately, half the load seemed to shed away. Things are still behind schedule, but the process has begun, and the motivation has started to come back.

A favourite text of scripture of mine that comes to me in low moments is from Isaiah (40:31) which says, ***'They that wait upon the Lord shall renew their strength, and mount up on wings as the eagle. They shall run, and not be weary; and they shall walk, and not faint.'*** I find it is valuable just to recall the words, and the strength that comes from remembering them.

But there are two other things we need to remember. Here in England the nights are starting to get lighter, the days warmer. We also get encouragement and renewal from the natural world as we see nature coming to life again.

May we look carefully at the things that motivate us, use all the gifts God has given us to bring about 'renewal of life and experience', and share with others things which can give them this encouragement – especially in their low moments, and times of need.

May we all find Lent a time of renewal and hope.

Thank you everyone for your Greetings on my 80th birthday. It was a very happy celebration.

April

Easter - a message of hope

Recently someone in a senior managerial post asked me how I thought people were reacting to the present economic climate, and the great reductions of jobs taking place, especially in public services. 'They feel numb and uncertain,' I replied.

This message is being prepared at the beginning of Holy Week as the story of Good Friday and Easter Day begins to unfold. It is a week of tension, betrayal, trial, and crucifixion. This situation *also* created a sense of numbness and uncertainty amongst the disciples of Jesus.

Good Friday with its horror of crucifixion, created a sense of shock in itself. We cannot overlook the fact that there was also a tremendous sense of trauma and loss amongst the first followers of Jesus caused by his death on the cross.

Easter Day however brings transformation. The women first at the tomb are bewildered at what has happened. An angel, seated at the entrance to the tomb says to them, 'Do not be afraid, for I know that you are looking for Jesus, who was crucified. *He is not here, he is risen.*' This gave the women great assurance and joy.

The story of the first Easter Day is one of eternal significance which expresses Christ's victory over sin and death.

My prayer for many who are suffering a sense of numbness and loss at the present time is that they may find encouragement from the Easter message too. May they find in Christ a message of hope that helps them through difficult days.

A Happy Easter and a time of blessing to all.

May

The Snooker Season

I'm not a great sports person but I do get hooked on snooker.

Some players are unequally matched. One romps ahead and wins; but there is always the player in some games who is losing, but perseveres. The leading scorer makes a mistake, often quite a trivial one, and the whole course of the game is changed; or maybe the loser sees that the only way forward requires some courageous stroke, a 'long shot' for instance, which succeeds, and the one who was losing wins.

Some aspects of snooker spell out to me what life is about.

Sometimes we are 'losing.' Everything is going against us, nothing is 'right', we haven't got as strong a grip on things as we used to have, others are getting on better than we are. We are tempted to 'give up'. These are natural reactions which most of us from time to time experience.

Does prayer have a role to play in winning through?

We must never forget that as long as we are involved in human affairs and relation-ships, there is a way through to a 'final result'. When we fail, we need to start again -many, many, times; and continue to live our lives as fully as we can to 'the glory of God'. Prayer, perseverance, persistence, and using the gifts we possess, all play their part.

Are we prepared, as it were, to 'fight the good fight', spiritually, so that 'in Christ' we may win through, and eventually discover what scriptures describe as our 'joy and eternal crown? '

Let us remember especially all who are going through difficult times as they persevere.

June

Holiday Conversations

We have just returned from our holidays, visiting Lake Garda and then a seven-day cruise in the Adriatic. It was the first time that we have ever been on such a holiday. We had good weather, good food, we travelled on the Costa Classica, there were no mishaps with the boat, and there was some fantastic scenery!

There were twenty-six in the group, and everyone seemed to gel well together.   We had many good conversations especially at mealtimes. Included in the party were a honeymoon couple, and a husband and wife who were celebrating 40 years of married life.

It is always fascinating to meet new people. You find many things in common, but you also discover many differences.

Some have special needs, and you would like to spend more time with them to talk through some of their issues. Others, on a one-to-one basis, share personal details about their lives and the problems they have experienced. Holidays for some can be valuable in this way. Perhaps we are able to give them some word of encouragement on life's journey.

When things have gone well on a trip you feel a sense of sadness when you finally say goodbye; in many cases you may never see them again.

'Lord, bless all those we meet for brief periods in our lives. May they too know fullness of life. In the name of Jesus Christ, our Lord. Amen.'

July

'Raise the stone and I am there!'

'The discovery of the Higgs 'bosun' particle', writes Ian Sample, 'ranks as one of the most important scientific advances of the past hundred years. *It proves there is an invisible energy field that pervades the vacuum of the known universe.'*

Professor Peter Higgs postulated the existence of this new particle nearly fifty years ago. Now in his eighties this former professor of physics from Edinburgh University is very happy with the verification of his theory.

One of the tabloid newspapers last week was headed 'Scientists prove the existence of ***'God' particle.'*** I misread the quotation marks, and read **'scientists prove existence of God'** particle.'

This is far too complex a subject to study in detail here, but it does raise the question: do we think of God as being 'over all', or of God being 'in all things?'

We believe that by His very nature God is both *'above all and* ***in all.****'*

A document of the early church called the Gospel of Thomas spoke of people finding God through Jesus in things around them, and records Jesus as saying 'Raise the stone, and there you will find me; cleave the wood, and there I am.'

We may not think like physicists in terms of 'particles', but we certainly do think of God as showing something of his nature through individual things; shall we say, trees and flowers, and all forms of life.

The discoveries of modern science can fill us with an even deeper sense of wonder. May we all recognise that God is at work even in the smallest 'particle' that has been discovered. In spite of difficult and hard things that happen.

We do live in an amazing and wonderful world.

August

May we all 'win through'

Many of us just now are deeply immersed in the Olympic Games. There is great excitement when someone wins a gold, silver or bronze medal; but we are sorry when some of our heroes fail to win.

Some competitors have too much attention in their build-up. This over-expectancy is crippling and destructive. The media, hungry for 'hype' and 'heroes', has made failure even more disappointing.

There is the world of difference between supporting others and creating an atmosphere of over-expectancy which does not allow for other factors to change the possibilities of success.

None of us can foretell the future for other people, whether it is with family or in the wider world events. We must also remember that the Olympics and life in general can bring us some pleasant surprises, where people 'win' against all odds - situations where we can be justly pleased.

My hope is that we will always give others support to reach their full potential, to 'win through'. Praying for others can be important too. We need to remember them in such a way that they may do well in ways that match their personalities, using the gifts that God has given.

Perhaps the most appropriate prayer that we can offer for them all is: *'Lord, we pray for the success of others, that they may be fulfilled in ways that are appropriate to their 'higher' natural inclinations and interests.'*

In the meantime, let us carry on enjoying the surprises of The Olympics, and admiring the skills of those who win.

Here in Britain, we are glad Team GB is doing so well.

P.S. On a personal note, you will be pleased to know that everything has gone well for the first yearly check-up after my operation.

September

Applauded for 'coming last'

This summer we've had a relentless roll of athletic activity with The Olympics, followed by the Paralympic games. The first is an event where the world's top athletes compete - men and women at the peak of body stamina and fitness. The

Paralympic games are also about competition, but from a very different point of view. They are about people who have overcome many different kinds of disabilities, injuries and setbacks yet who remain determined to do well and succeed.

The Paralympic sprinter *Ben Rushgrove said, "My philosophy is never to think what I can't do - only what I can."* He is a reminder to us that we can all 'hide' behind what we feel we can't do, and as a result miss out on any kind of personal fulfilment. The Ben Rushgroves of this world should be our real role models and not world 'celebs.' What grief people find by trying to imitate false models of success.

One 1500 metres distance runner in the Paralympics, was a role model 'supremo'. I cannot remember where he came from - one of the African countries I believe. He was of slight build, had lost one of his arms, and he completed the race *seven minutes* after everyone else.

As he trundled along the last stretch 80,000 people at the stadium, moved with great emotion, gave him a tremendous heartfelt cheer as he crossed the finishing line. It was a moment never to be forgotten. This Paralympic experience reminds me of the words we find in one of our hymns by Charles Wesley which says:

'O that each from His Lord,

May receive the glad word

Well and faithfully done.'

Ultimately, faithful living is not about the acclaim of the crowd, but receiving the 'joy' and acclamation of the Lord.

May everyone respond faithfully to their challenge. Life's not about 'competitive winning', but 'faithfully completing.'

May we have the wisdom and grace to live in this way.

October

Leadership does make a difference

Last week I went to the biennial conference of the National Association of Chaplains to the Police. It's the first time that I've been although I have served as a police chaplain for thirteen years.

There were nearly a hundred of us there at this inspiring event from constabularies from all over England, Wales and Scotland. It was a very poignant time to meet so soon after the murder of two women police officers in the greater Manchester area. The funeral of one of them was taking place while we were there and the second one shortly after we left our conference at Swanwick. We remembered these officers with our own two minutes of silence. Although very few of us had met each other before it was amazing to find out how much we had in common. In every situation we have found our role increasingly important, especially with all the cutbacks that are taking place in policing. The chaplain is seen as someone with a caring but impartial role.

There was one area however of growing overall concern: the appointment of Police and Crime Commissioners for every police force in the country (PCCs). This will change policing tremendously. How important it will be for the right people to be chosen to fulfil these tasks.

As the president of our Police Chaplains Association reminded us, we should pray about this matter and encourage people to vote for those who are best equipped to do this extremely important work.

November

Be thankful for serial ('cereal') choices

I'm sure that all of us feel we are living in times of tremendous change, and we are often called upon to make decisions on all kinds of things that previously we would have taken for granted.

Yesterday we were shopping in the supermarket and needed cereals. There was a choice of over 30 cereals all packaged differently. Then on the other side of the aisle another selection was headed 'adult' cereals. Even more choices to make!

However, we always live in times of change. 'Nothing ever stays still' said the Greek philosopher. Everything is in a state of flux. The question is: how do we cope with it?

We have to try and keep abreast of things; but we also have to say to ourselves, do we really value what we already possess, and do we appreciate the many choices that we are given?

We have to cultivate a sense of thankfulness for variety and choice. In a very practical way, we can show this by saying ‘thank you’ to people in our families or community friendship circles, and the hosts of people who help us and serve us in the wider society too. All bring variety and choice to our lives.

Perhaps then we can more naturally say ‘thank you’ to God for all the good things that we have received, and give support to those who needs are greater than our own.

In the business and bustle of ‘change’, let us be thankful for choice, and all who provide it.

December

Light for ‘people walking in darkness’

This message is being prepared on the day after the winter solstice in the ‘northern’ hemisphere, the darkest day of the year! Today there is a steady downpour of rain, and all over the country there are those who are being flooded - with all the restrictions, losses and damage that this creates.

For many, these are gloomy days economically. There is much sad news. The tragic shooting of children and teachers in America, the fearful situation in war-torn Syria, and all kinds of people in many parts of the world who are struggling to live. We also remember people around us in this time of year who are feeling the loss of loved ones, and breakdowns in relationships. We need to remember them all in our prayers.

It was in a very gloomy situation, like this for many today, that the prophet Isaiah wrote these words, 'A people walking in darkness have seen a great light.'

Here God tells a hard-hit people about a Messiah, who will bring joy, peace and prosperity to a weary people. This verse of Scripture is often used in carol services to remind us of the coming of Jesus: not to bring exactly the kind of Kingdom that Isaiah expected perhaps, but certainly to be present amongst people as the 'Light of the world.'

We thankfully celebrate His coming, for it is in Christ's Birth that God brings hope to all human-kind.

May the joy of Christmas be with us during this Holy Season of the year, and may the New Year bring hope, 'light' and a better future to all in need.

Thanks for contributions via email, and welcome to newcomers. Pauline joins me in wishing every-one a joyful and peaceful Christmas, and a Happy New Year.

Chapter 3: 2013 - Before the storm

A quiet year, full of things that many people in their late seventies and early eighties might still enjoy doing - looking after the garden, meeting people, keeping in touch with the family, supporting church events, good causes, concerts, holidays, U3A, enjoying taking part in sporting activities, entertaining friends, volunteering, still helping in the pastoral work of the local churches, and hoping for good things politically to happen in our country and in the world.

There are great variations in our life-cycle. Some in their mid-50s are talking about retirement, but others are active even in their late 90s. Part of the secret, health permitting, is in actively learning a variety of new things. Ball games were never my forte. At school I went cross-country running instead. In retirement however some friends who were really good at table tennis encouraged me to play. One in particular helped me tremendously to improve. So much so that in time I could hold my own and sometimes even win! It remains important however to keep active as long as we can in every kind of activity because the saying 'if you don't use it you lose it' certainly has some truth in it.

January

'Life-long logistics!'

Sometimes it seems almost impossible to 'get going'. So many things come along and interrupt us.

We feel robbed of opportunities to 'settle down' to what we really want to do. When we feel the moment has arrived however to do the things we ought to do, we must seize it.

Interruptions might bring new openings, and opportunities can be 'sent' to help us to lead a fuller life. It is often difficult though to know the difference between a distraction and a new opportunity. May we have 'the wisdom' to know the difference, but if we are trying to live 'by faith' there are moments when we have to take risks and travel along unfamiliar paths.

Time will tell of course whether the decisions we make are the right ones, but we must always persevere to follow what Charles Wesley would call ‘our providential way’.

As we remember friends going through difficult times, in health or in relationships, as well as those who are getting on well, my prayer is that we may all open ‘new doors’ in the New Year, as well as maintaining many long-term friendships and opportunities.

May the year ahead be one in which we all find strength and support on our journey.

February

We are not the centre of the world

Not one of us is 'the centre of the world.' Yet we often live and think as if we are!

It not only applies to us as individuals, but as families, communities, religious and ethnic groups, and nations too.

This is a good starting point for us to begin thinking about Lent. Traditionally, after Shrove Tuesday or Pancake Day, we come to Ash Wednesday which is basically thought of as a day of penitence. There are those who begin to deny themselves of all kinds of things, believing that in doing so they will enter into a deeper meaning of 'serving God.'

It is a good thing for us all to practise forms of self-denial during this season, but at times something far trickier is required from us. Can we break ourselves of the habit of making ourselves 'the centre of the world?'

This is far more difficult than we might imagine. It means listening carefully to what other people are saying, and not just wanting our own way. It means recognising the validity of other people's point of view, and making allowances for what they are thinking and the way that they are living. Anything that we see that is good in others we should be encouraging, and not hastily condemning anything that is 'foreign' to us.

Paradoxically, although Jesus is at the centre of our faith, he does not see himself as being at the centre of worldly power, as Satan tempts him to be.

In His greatness, he comes as a servant, and bears the burdens of others, and not to be the centre of attention.

The question is: are we willing to follow his example?

May His Peace be with us all.

April

Jesus and eternal life

This Easter message is being prepared during one of the worst snow-ups for 50 years. Last week was the beginning of Spring; but we have gone back to Winter instead!

In nature things do not always progress automatically from one stage to another. In the seasons of many people's lives too there are many periods when things do not go smoothly. Hardship and tragedy are the experience of many people as they move through their stages of life. During difficult times they need our support and prayers.

In this week, Holy Week, the triumph of Palm Sunday leads through to the humiliation of Good Friday and the glory of Easter Day.

Because of his divine calling, Jesus had to 'face the music', the forces of evil. He was put on trial, but no real case was made against him. He suffered insults, all the pain of a cruel death, and was crucified on a cross between two thieves.

Good Friday is central to our faith, because we believe that Jesus died 'to make us good'. He is the One through whom our sins are forgiven.

Just as 'winter' however eventually progresses through to 'spring' and regeneration, so Jesus passes through 'death' to 'new life'.

The message of Easter Day is Resurrection. 'He is not here, he is risen' is the message that the women hear from the angels. We too are reminded that Christ's death is not the end, but to those who believe in him it is the progression to a 'new beginning,' a new 'spring.' Jesus' resurrection opens up another stage on the way to 'eternal life.'

May we all find great joy and hope in this.

Pauline joins me in wishing you all a very Happy Easter!

May

Does 'reality continue to ruin our lives?'

The shuttering of an empty shop in Nottingham has these words daubed on it: *'Reality continues to ruin my life.'*

What did the writer have in mind? Perhaps the shopkeeper had tried hard to build up a business in these times of severe recession. Maybe his product failed to match up to those of rivals in the neighbourhood, or family circumstances made it impossible to carry on.

Circumstances can make it very difficult to 'get out of the slimy pit' and the 'miry clay' as the Psalmist would say. Many on a downward 'slippery-slope' do find it very difficult to think positively and progressively.

However, many situations that we think are hopeless do have possibilities for change. It may simply be that those suffering losses just now need others to be aware of their plight. Do we spend enough time talking to people who are struggling to exist? A listening ear linked with practical support can make a tremendous difference.

We need to give help and prayerful support to all kinds of people who are struggling at the present time. In the wider sphere for instance we remember at this week - **Christian Aid week** - a straightforward way in which we can generously give.

These times of crisis and stress provide us with God-given opportunities to help. What we do may actually be the 'reality' that brings them relief. St. Paul said to the Galatians: 'Do not grow weary in doing good.' May we also follow this advice in helping others.

June

The Queen's Coronation

(Forgive this month's letter taking the form of a personal reminiscence, but....!)

A favourite question on many local radio stations at the moment is this: 'If you were around, what were you doing at the time of the Queen's Coronation 60 years ago?'

My experience was memorable in an unexpected way!

I was doing my National service, at HQ Southern Command, Wilton, near Salisbury. I used to play a small Church organ mid-week at the small parish church of St. Peters in Fugglestone near Wilton. After we had finished our work for the day, a small intimate group of four or five of us used to meet there during the week and share in the evening service of Compline together. To me it was a very moving place to worship in, because it had been the church where George Herbert, poet and priest, had ministered centuries before.

Prior to National Service, all through my teens, I had regularly played a harmonium at two of the small mid-week meetings of the Young Men's Bible class at Vicar Street Methodist Church, in Dudley. Quite a large number of us, incidentally, who belonged to this Class became Ministers, and Local Preachers in the Methodist Church. The Queen's Coronation however presented me with a sudden unexpected musical challenge to which I had to make a response.

The parish church to which St. Peters was attached, were holding a special thanksgiving service to celebrate the Queen's Coronation. The organist due to play was taken ill. I was asked at very short notice, if I would play.

It was a big and important event for the church. I think there were about 250 people there, although I didn't count them. There was a large pipe organ with a tremendous number of stops and several manuals to cope with - a daunting, rather petrifying task, especially as I had never been trained as an organist!

Some of the simpler hymns went fine. With others I struggled, and made quite a few mistakes. I still squirm when I think of my efforts at that service. But there were two redeeming features. The choir and the congregation sang really heartily, and drowned many of my faults, and many of course realised that I had only stepped in because of an emergency!

It was rather an unusual way of serving 'Queen and country' at that very special and significant time!

July

'Surviving or thriving?'

When visiting a police station as chaplain, conversations often begin like this: 'Are you surviving or thriving?'

When I ask how they would rate their answers, on a basis of one to ten, several may well say, (light heartedly) 'minus one!'

Most of us during the course of a day either consciously or unconsciously weigh up how we are getting on. At the end of the day we may well say to God in our prayers something along the lines of the General Confession which says 'We have left undone those things which we ought to have done; and we have done those things which we ought not to have done; and there is no health in us.'

From what we might call the 'human endeavour' side of things, we all desire to make some progress along the way that opens up before us, a way that we travel in many parts of the journey with other people, and we ask for forgiveness of our failures.

We may feel sometimes however that in spite of our best efforts, our loads may burden us down. This is surely the point at which 'faith' truly comes in.

Jesus says '***Come*** unto me, ***all you*** that labour and are ***heavy laden***, and I will give you rest. Take my yoke upon you and learn of me; for I am meek and lowly in heart.' (Matthew 11:28)

These words apply to our working-life as well as other situations. This does not mean that we will have no burdens to carry, but rather they are lightened as we trust in Christ. For He is the one who willingly accompanies us on the journey, providing rest and refreshment that makes burden-carrying possible.

My hope is that all of us are somewhere on the 'surviving plus' side of things. May we in all life's scenes learn how to trust God through Jesus far more than we have ever done before!

The Nottinghamshire Police Chaplaincy Team in 2017
(L to R: David Monkton, Paul Wright, David Henson)

August

'There is no gain without pain'

Just now much of Nottingham is in turmoil. The station is closed for five weeks for modernisation. Passengers, who normally travel by train, are travelling by bus to outlying stations, and many taxi drivers are having a difficult time finding places to pick up passengers.

The manager of the railway station has apologised publicly, and has assured people that the changes will make a tremendous improvement but, he says, 'there is no gain without pain.' The alterations will make things so much better for our city and travellers through it.

'There is no gain without pain,' is a valuable catchphrase, and I wonder whether we see the significance of it in other walks of life?

There is a great deal wrong in modern society. Pollution of many different kinds is seriously damaging our environment and every form of life of within it. There is great inequality of wealth, and many totalitarian regimes exist which makes the lives of billions of people extremely fearful and miserable.

As individuals and as world citizens we have to remember that there can be 'no gain without pain,' as there can be no improvement without a willingness of all to make sacrifices for others. Are we prepared for example to live more sensitive lifestyles that are less wasteful and more considerate of the needy peoples of the world and even for human existence itself?

From a Christian viewpoint we wait for the kingdom of God to come, but it's coming is not going to be easy. Jesus says it is going to be like the pangs of a new birth before new life can begin.

There is an urgent challenge to live in such a way that we have the well-being of 'all people' at heart.

May we all persevere happily and prayerfully striving for this 'better way.' Jesus calls us every time we pray the Lord's Prayer, to work and pray that God's kingdom will come on earth as it is in heaven.

September

Religion and Life

One of our readers recently sent a quote from 'The Times' originating from a Church newsletter.

"Religion has generated not only great architecture and art, but a framework within which to eat, celebrate and grieve together. Its rituals are deliberately soothing. It offers a code of etiquette defining how to behave - something modern libertarians rail against..."

There is much in this quotation that rings true. We do need a framework in which to 'eat, celebrate and grieve together' and 'rituals' that are 'deliberately soothing.'

'Religion' in spite of its abuse, does offer a 'code of etiquette defining how to behave'. We ignore these codes of behaviour, built up over many centuries, at our peril.

This does not mean however that life patterns always have to stay the same. Our environment, and rapid changes taking place in society frequently compel us to revise the way we view life, especially when we carefully consider what 'loving and caring for others' is all about. Even ancient practices, based on limited understandings of life and health have to be challenged and changed.

On the other hand, 'modern libertarians' have frequently lost the plot. Only time will tell, of course, but ultimately, we believe they give an unsatisfactory answer to what life is all about.

The prophet (Micah, 6:8) says:

'What does the Lord require of you? Do justly, love kindness, and walk humbly with your God.'

The prophet's 'code', might well provide a common framework for people of many different outlooks to follow.

October

Crabbed age and 'being cool'

'Crabbed age and youth cannot live together' writes Shakespeare. 'Youth is full of pleasance, age is full of care'.

Old people can be crabby, especially when they are going through frustrating times; but young people can also be crabby, especially as they struggle towards maturity.

Recently after leading a Sunday morning service, a teenage girl said: 'Thank you for the service, it was really cool!' This made my day! I wasn't particularly speaking to young people present, but felt very encouraged to have said something that had some resonance with a young member of the congregation.

Giving guidance to others can be very valuable but how important careful listening is as well. The young and the elderly need to listen to each other because in very different ways they are going through times of change. Both ages can be dogmatic, but also mutually supportive. Real wisdom includes listening from both ends of the age-spectrum, and bearing in mind the needs of those 'in between' as well.

All need to reach towards maturity of understanding in whatever walks of life they are involved. Church, family, community and global concerns especially require a commitment from us to listen and share in order to feel 'at one' with each other.

The prophet Joel envisages God, saying, ‘I will pour out My Spirit on all humanity; then your sons and your daughters will prophesy, your old men will have dreams, and your young men will see visions.’

We had a first glimpse of this on the Day of Pentecost. May the day quickly come when all ages will share their dreams and visions together.

November

Information overload and our real treasure

Recently our cooker went wrong, and we had to buy a new one because we could not find replacement parts. When the new cooker was installed, we received a book of instructions with 48 pages in it!

This is one of the nightmares of present-day living. Almost everything new that you buy has a whole list of do’s and don'ts.

We are all suffering from 'information overload.' If we do not get a thing right first time, the mistake can take hours to sort out and leave us with a sense of frustration.

There is a new illness called 'digital fatigue,’ and it has very little to do with ‘tired fingers’ except that many people have to spend excessive time with computers in order to do their work. This is a serious problem.

There are many of my ministerial friends for instance who find their ability to get on with their pastoral work is seriously curtailed by all the extra work that centralised bureaucracy has created in this sphere.

Mark Vernon reminds us that new medical research suggests that 'the heart is more than a physical pump. It interacts with the human spirit. Brain and heart work in tandem, not as master and slave.'

We all have to take great care that we do not allow the tremendous demands of digital technology to drive our lives. Brain and heart must work in tandem. The question is: have we got the balance right?

Jesus reminds us that ‘where your heart is, there is your treasure also.' (Matthew 6:21)

Do we allow the deeper the affairs of the heart and our desire to seek the greater good, real space in our time and prayers?

December

Earliest experiences of Christmas

What is your earliest experience of Christmas?

Mine is going to bed on Christmas Eve, dropping off to sleep very quickly, waking up very early, and feeling down the bottom of the bed to find out whether Father Christmas had filled my stocking!

Usually there was an apple, an orange, a selection of unshelled nuts and neatly wrapped little presents - not fully recognised until the full break of day. A larger sized present might be waiting down-stairs.

The Christmas cake, the pudding, a large chicken, crackers, a trifle, the Christmas tree, the room decorations together with holly and ivy, all added to the excitement.

Many of these things still play a very large part in our celebration of Christmas, but how important it is to keep a sense of wonder with it all!

An ancient Carol begins with the words 'A Great and Mighty Wonder.' That's just what Christmas is, however we celebrate it. The birth of Jesus is at the centre, for in the coming of Jesus we believe that God brings hope to a world that struggles to find it.

Whatever outlook we have on life, may we never lose this child-like quality. Even although we have to grow up and mature, 'wonder' should still remain a quality that we preserve, value, and 'hold on' to.

Pauline joins me in wishing everyone a Peaceful Christmas and a Happy New Year.

Chapter 4: 2014.

Prayer, loss, and our friends

When starting to put these letters together, I soon discovered how difficult it was to share my inner thoughts. Following successful surgery for a bowel cancer there was the sudden and unexpected loss of Pauline, then coping with a bladder cancer three months later, and the ageing process which of course affects us all. All these things brought with them turmoil, changing lifestyle and personal needs.

Pauline and I had been married nearly 54 years. Our union had been a very close one. We met in Coventry, drawn together by our involvement with concerns for the West Indians and Pakistanis arriving in large numbers in the community. On marrying, we served in East London, our eldest child being born within the sound of Bow Bells. Then followed Saffron Walden in rural Essex, Lincoln, the Shetland Islands (eleven years), and then nine years in St Albans before retiring to Nottingham. We were contrasting personalities and occasionally we had to work hard to find common ground, often on issues that on looking back do not seem so important. All of us have moments when we think of things we could have done a lot better. At times we may feel we have miserably failed, but these things have often helped us to forge an extremely meaningful, stable, and loving caring partnership for which we can be deeply thankful.

Many neighbours, friends and the churches I go to conduct worship at, have helped. Although my family do not live nearby, they keep in touch frequently. The fellowship and prayers of people have meant a great deal to me as well as courses on bereavement and other forms of caring. It has not been easy, but strangely enough I have found fresh dimensions of experience of all kinds during this painful time. New perspectives not only give us insight into our own limitations but also into pastoral care. It is probably true to say that we can only enter into the bereavement experience of other people and friends when we have experienced close personal loss ourselves. Even then everyone is affected differently with many different patterns of loss.

Our last visit to Woodthorpe Park.

Every step was precious.

First, hand-in-hand, then arm in arm.

We walked past bushes, winter flowers and trees.

The last time before her departure -

A glimpse of the Garden of Eden -

With a comforting breeze.

Woodthorpe Park

January

Looking at the New Year

A New Year hymn written by Charles Wesley begins: 'Come let us anew our journey pursue.'

The New Year for many is not so much about making new resolutions but simply resolving to 'do things better' the next time; but there may be some key points where things need altering because of changing circumstances in our lives, or to those closest to us. This includes such things as leaving home for the first time, going away to work or study, entering into a new relationship, getting married, the arrival of children, children leaving home, economic difficulties, unemployment, retirement, bereavement, or reaching a 'significant age' when we have to remember that our life-spans do not go on indefinitely! All these things need careful thought.

Prayer, contemplation and reflection will all have an important part to play. We often need to share our concerns with friends, and there is the need to be life-long learners too.

We also have to bear in mind, that our lives are not self-contained. We are not the centre of the world and we have a great responsibility towards all other people within it. In the Bible we are reminded that after worshipping God, loving our neighbours is as important as our own well-being!

I would like to wish everyone 'a good year ahead' as we continue 'anew' life's journey.

February

Letting part of our past go

At the present time I need to 'de-clutter.' I have accumulated such a large number of magazines, books, notes and jottings, making it difficult to find things essentially needed to do things I really ought to do.

One thing I did manage to do however was to dispose of about 30 years of sermon notes! Would posterity have made any use of them? I don't think so, firstly because it is doubtful whether other people would be able to read my writing, and secondly it is questionable whether many would be relevant to preaching today.

There was a sense of relief at letting them go.

Nevertheless, there are still prayers that have been written, and detailed diaries covering such a tremendous variety of experiences both of Ministry and many other things we have shared together. There is also a great deal of other material that ought to be discarded.

Getting rid of 'baggage' is important. To do so gives us more freedom. Our life pilgrimage is likened by St Paul to a race where we need to cast on one side every unnecessary load.

Are we continuing to learn how to travel lightly?

This includes dropping the baggage of resentments of whatever kind these might be because there is always so much more to be thankful for. It seems to me that true wisdom begins here for all of us, at whatever age we may be.

Every blessing, especially to all who are finding themselves in any kind of distress due to the weather.

P.S. Just before Christmas, the University of Nottingham Theology Department asked me to take part in an informal conversation on Methodist spirituality. If you would like to see this on U-tube, Google the "Rev Dr David Monkton" on the subject "Why study Methodist spirituality?".

March

Pancakes and the season of Lent

To the best of my knowledge, it's the first time I've written this monthly newsletter on Pancake Day. About an hour or so ago Pauline and I made and enjoyed eating our pancakes. It's a bit of a joint effort really: Pauline putting all the ingredients together and putting the contents in the frying pan. I take a hand thoroughly beating the batter, and then occasionally trying to toss them. It's only very rarely that I succeed!

Traditionally, Pancake Day is a day of preparation for Lent.

We frequently think of Lent as a time when we examine ourselves as individuals before God, like Jesus himself who spent forty days in the wilderness being tested and 'tried out'. Very few of us venture into a 'wilderness' experience in the way that he did, but we do make some attempt to recognise the importance of 'giving more time to God' at this time of the year.

Pancake Day however also reminds us that Lent is something that we take part in corporately, together with other people who serve God in the name of Jesus. Through doing this we believe that we can discover some ways in which our lives can be better fitted in service for the kingdom of God.

May every one of us find ourselves better fitted to serve God, and serve others.

P.S. It's come as a bombshell, completely out of the blue, but a week last Sunday, Pauline had a small stroke, and spent three days in hospital. Her speech is now much better, she is resting well and making good progress. We would value your prayerful support at this time.

April

Pauline, and Easter

Sadly, Pauline died in hospital yesterday. Thankfully most of us were able to be with her within minutes of the hospital call. Fortunately, she did not have a great deal of pain, and the gravity of her illness behind her strokes had only been known for a short time, but it has all happened so quickly.

Because of the advanced state of her illness, I naturally made other arrangements for any fixed engagements so that I could be with her whenever the moment of greatest need might be, so this year for the first time in the whole of my ministry of over fifty years I will not be presiding at any of the Easter Day communion services. Pauline was always present in the congregation with me at the early morning service.

I shall miss leading the declaration at the beginning of the Easter Day Service where the preacher says 'The Lord is Risen' and the congregation replies 'He is risen indeed!'
On the other hand, how important the words of

the Easter Promise are in themselves - whoever says them! Jesus in his risen power says to all who simply trust in Him, and are in special need, 'because I live, you will live also.'

We find great comfort and support in these words.

Thank you for remembering us in your thoughts and prayers. It is deeply appreciated.
In the meantime I'm sure my family too will also share with me in wishing you a time of meaningful meditation on Good Friday, and a very Happy Easter.

May

The support of friends.....

First of all, thank you to everyone who has given such tremendous support over the last two months. Just now, I am unable to respond individually, but simply want to say how moved we have been by the tributes to Pauline, your prayers and your personal support which has given us a great deal of comfort in our loss.

Many say 'Be very gentle with yourself,' or 'Don't try and do too much. Take your time, and have plenty of rest.' This is all good advice in a time of great adjustment.

Others may say, 'Call in and see us and have a coffee or a meal with us,' or 'If there is any way in which we can help please let us know.'

It seems to me that it is important, wherever possible, to take up the help that other people want to give; not only for our own sake, but also for the sake of the people who are offering too. It helps them to feel part of what is happening to us.

Equally important though, through our 'giving' and 'taking', we help to strengthen what real community and friendship is all about, and gives us some idea what it really means for people to be 'the salt of the earth.'

With all good wishes, every blessing, and thank you again.

June

Hospitals and our well-being,

Hospitals have changed tremendously in recent years. This came over strongly when preparing these notes whilst in hospital last week. When you see the doctors, nurses, administrators and all those who have specialist roles to look after us, you couldn't find a more cosmopolitan group of people anywhere!

In contrast, many hospital patients have lived in the Nottingham area all their lives. A number of the conversations however, apart from those naturally wanting to talk about their illnesses, were about their concerns over changes that were taking place in our society. Particularly strong views were expressed by those feeling threatened by what they saw as a loss of 'British' identity.

There is one thing certain however: we cannot go back to where we were! Today we live in what Marshall McLuhan was fond of calling a 'global village.' The digital age makes the world even more so. The question is not 'how do we preserve our identity?' but 'how do we build a new one?'

This is the great challenge. In a rapidly changing world, we cannot live in our own little corners. We all have our part to play in the 'global community' to see that justice, kindness and compassion is shown to all.

The parable of the good Samaritan that Jesus told, dwelt on this very important point, and it is good for us all to remember this. May we be willing to show compassion to all kinds of people!

With all good wishes, and every blessing.

P.S. Thanks to all who have given such great support during the last three months. It is deeply appreciated. You will be pleased to know that the surgery on my bladder last Tuesday was successful and that I am making a good recovery. Kind regards, D.

July

Not winning but good batting

Last week Nottingham was a different city. The test match was on against India. Although England didn't win, a remarkable achievement took place. The two closing batsmen achieved an all-time record score in their partnership of 198 runs, and it was achieved by two batsmen who were rather an unusual combination. One was a good run scorer, but the other was a fast bowler and not a batsman at all! Previously around 30 runs was the highest score he had made in professional cricket. This time he scored 81 runs!

I thought this was a wonderful story, and a reminder to us how sometimes unexpected people can achieve great things in unexpected ways. It was the case of a good batsmen having someone at the 'other end' who first of all was 'simply there.' However, in the circumstances, the 'inferior' batsman was stimulated to achieve extraordinary results.

Most of us look at the world almost in despair and think that the world's problems are so vast and insurmountable. However, let us not look on in exasperation. Although there are many things that are deeply worrying in the world, let us not rule out the possibility that we all may have some significant part to play in seeing the world changed, even although we feel our role in it is not a brilliant one.

We need to pray for good leaders in the world. Once we spot these people, we must give them all the support that we can with our prayers, and in practical ways as well, wherever we can. In this way we can 'play alongside' those who have the ability to do great things. Through their care for humanity they can achieve those things which we often describe as 'working for the kingdom of God,' and we too can play an effective part.

P.S. Thank you all for your continued support. It means a great deal to me at this time.

September

So(u)(le)s are hee(a)led here

A church in Derby had a word 'pun' on its church notice board which read as follows: "So(u)l(e)s are hee(a)led here.' It was a clumsy pun really, but it was trying to make an important point. Part of the mission of the Christian church is to bring healing into people's lives, just like cobblers (used to) repair shoes.

Jesus saw the importance of the dignity that men and women should find in their lives. Yes, we are sinners, we all have faults and shortcomings; but the work of Jesus was also about restoring men and women to what God wanted them to be. Jesus was also seen as the gentle healer. 'The bruised reed he will not break' says one verse of Scripture. He came to 'bind up' the broken hearted, and to release people from things that keep them back.

If we are his followers this is our work too. A twitter-quip recently said: 'Never look down on anybody unless you're helping them Up.' That's how it should be.

Modern commerce works on the principle that we live in a 'throw-away' society; that when things are broken, we simply buy a new product. Many people feel that their lives are like that too; that they have been discarded and looked upon as being useless. Part of our task is to help repair broken situations.

The Good News is, that if we truly follow Jesus Christ, we are sharing in this transforming work. May we all explore carefully ways in which we can carry out our task, our calling. We might even be doing His work without knowing it!

October

'You only stay balanced if you keep going forward'

A keen cyclist recently twittered: 'if you want to keep your balance on a cycle, you need to go forward.' When you apply this to life as a whole, it is a profound remark.

Balance is extremely important. There has to be some kind of balance in everything that we do. Sometimes there is lots of talk and no action. How easy it is when this happens to lose any real sense of balance. Without action so many of our theories about how we should live become irrelevant, because they have never been tested.

There are times when we feel in the doldrums. There is no wind in our sails. This often happens in times of stress and trauma. It may take some time to get a sense of balance and forwardness going again.

There is however a kind of healing in 'getting the balance right' as we start going forward. I'm reminded of the words of Jesus where he says to the man who is sick, waiting at the Pool of Bethesda for a chance to be healed: 'Take up your bed and walk.' Although Jesus gives the command, the healing action has to be performed by the man himself.

Sometimes for all of us, healing comes as we go forward in faith. We too, need to take up our beds (or mattresses!) and start going forward. Getting the 'balance right' or 'healing' cannot be separated from the action of actually making a move forward ourselves.

May we all go forward 'in faith' whatever our outlook may be. There is that idealistic opportunity or practical task that we feel we ought to venture into. Seize the moment, and in working a new venture out, may we find blessings that will bring a sense of wholeness to us all.

P.S. Thanks for all enquiries about my 'well-being.' The going is still raw and slow at times, but the results of my surgery check up are very good, and I don't have to go again to hospital for six months.

November

Harmony, togetherness, and the ukulele band

The recent visit of the Nottinghamshire Ukulele Band to Mapperley Methodist Church was a very moving event. I was particularly taken with their playing and singing of Aida's 'March of the Hebrew slaves' and their version of John Greenleaf Whittier's hymn 'Dear Lord and Father of mankind forgive our foolish ways.'

I think of the ukulele as a very basic instrument with a very humble origin. In a string band they have an enchanting and hypnotic effect - created simply by the players strumming in time and in tune together.

Behind this sense of 'togetherness' there something that is important for us all to experience. The world needs people of very humble origin as well as the privileged, to seek ways in which they can be banded together to bring harmony, for this can be of tremendous therapeutic value for us all - even if we are just listeners.

The more 'togetherness' that we are able to get with those who are around us, and between the nations of the world, the happier we are all going to be. Much loneliness, isolation and misunderstanding and fear in society will disappear. We will even discover a fuller meaning of the word 'peace.'

May we all practice the skills of togetherness that can bring harmony and peace in the world. In so doing we will be responding to the request of the Psalmist, who tells us to 'seek peace and pursue it.'

May we all gain inspiration from the sense of belonging together that is found in a ukulele band!

Mapperley Ukulele Band

Practice Night at a local Baptist Church

December

Christingles and Christmas

After taking the Christingle service at my local Methodist Church, someone said, 'That's a service for children isn't it?' Yes, originally it was, and it is very popular even among children today.

At the service I took on Monday afternoon however everyone was much older - at least in the 65 to 95 age range - but everyone received a Christingle, consisting of an orange with a red band around it, a candle representing Christ as the light of the world placed on the top of the orange, and small bits of fruit on sticks inserted into the orange representing 'the fruits of the earth.'

After the candles were lit and at the close of our time of worship, I had to say 'Go, in the power of The Spirit to bring light to others,' then we all closed with the words, *'Praise to Christ our light!'*

These closing words are rich with symbolism. All of us, of whatever age we are, should 'go out' into the world 'in the power of The Spirit to bring light to others.' As Christians we do so, because 'Christ is our light', and we believe that Jesus is 'the light of the world.'

Whatever our outlook may be, may we know the peace of Christ, in a world desperately needing to shake off 'darkness', and live in the light that God intended us all to share in.

Two lines from one of Charles Wesley's carols sums it up well, when he says, 'Life and light to all He brings, risen with healing in his wings.'

Let us pray that all may have 'light and life' this Christmas time.

Wishing you all a peaceful and blessed Christmas, and a Happy New Year.

Chapter 5: 2015

Taking things a bit at a time

This has been a 'nibbling along' year. Naturally the shock of sudden bereavement, its deep emotional moments and surgery can leave us with periods of great uncertainty, times of many phobias and 'two steps forward and one step back' experiences....

It was great to go to New Zealand for the first time with my sister to see our brother and meet several members of his family whom I had never got to know before. My brother has been there 40 years. Whilst wondering whether I would cope with the journey I was so glad we went. It was great to experience so much that was new, beautiful, and unexpected in the countryside.

It takes time to put an anthology together. Sometimes moments of rapid compiling, other times of doubting the reality of doing it. But I have found that writing can be a therapy in itself! All the way through our lives however we can really only live by having some kind of faith to take us along 'even like a little grain of mustard seed' says Jesus. A great part of calling to ministry is encouraging others to live by faith.

Articles on various aspects of well-being are very popular just now. Often, they have something very worthwhile to say; but frameworks of well-being are useless unless underneath there is something that speaks louder than articles about it. Faith is needed in some form or another at the rock bottom of our being.

'By faith' Jesus tells us we can move mountains, but in practice we can only move many mountains slowly. It seems to me that often have to go along nibbling in faith, frequently a day at a time.

A children's talk that I often gave much earlier in my ministry was the fairy story of a clockmaker who made a very special clock.

'When he finished making the clock he said, 'I want you to strike a million times.' He then left his workshop and closed the door.

The newly made clock started to cry, 'I have to strike a million times, however shall I do it?'

The grandfather clock sitting in the corner of the workshop said, 'don't worry my dear. First of all, strike once at 1 o'clock, two times at 2 o'clock, three times at 3 o'clock, four times 4 o'clock, and at every quarter of an hour. Do this throughout the day....and when you get to 12 o'clock, start again, and you will strike a million times easily.'

A rather quaint story. I'm sure I have learnt a lot from it myself!

Up Helly Aa, the Viking Fire Festival procession,
begins outside the Methodist Church
in Lerwick, The Shetland Islands

(Mid) January

Growth and change have already begun

This time of the year for many is notoriously 'heavy going.'

The coldness, the dark nights, and generally miserable weather can make people feel ill, and even depressed, so it is understandable that people do many different things to liven up their winter months.

Outside the Manse where we lived when we were in Shetland, was the starting point for the 'Up Helly Aa' Viking Festival. It was a marvellous sight to see up to 900 men in procession with large burning torches, marching to a special place where the replica of a Viking boat was set alight by their torches. The blaze lit up the dark winter night. Every year it comes as a welcome and entertaining break in the dark winter months and is a symbol to remind people there that after the winter solstice, lighter days cannot be far behind.

However, there are many different kinds of things that help us to cope with the hardness of the winter season. Observation of the natural world can be a great source of help and encouragement. It is really marvellous, for instance, to see in our gardens, that buds are already appearing on the bushes, and bulbs are starting to push their shoots through the ground even when the cold and darkness are at their worst.

It is helpful for us all to remember, that when we are going through cold, dark and difficult days, growth and change is already starting to take place, and as we go forward in faith we discover that these things remind us that the hope of brighter days ahead can certainly help us along our way!

February

Give us today our daily bread

Catering for one, especially if you are not used to it, is not easy!

In the preparation of meals, you are always free to try out new ideas, and if it doesn't work, there is only one person disappointed! Supermarket shopping for food for everyone, however, has its hazards. 'Two for the price of one' or two items at a reduced cost means there is a danger of hoarding food, or eating more than we really need.

When the children of Israel were in the wilderness, we are told, special provision was made for them with 'bread from heaven', called 'manna', but they are only to gather up enough just for each day - the only exception being that they are to collect an extra supply on the sixth day for The Sabbath.

Those who gathered more than they needed found that the next day it was 'full of worms and smelt rotten', and Moses their leader was angry with them!

Isn't there a danger that we too, like the Israelites, can stockpile food when we shouldn't?

I would suggest that we need to bear this in mind during Lent, and ask the question: do we spend money on food that we do not need, and forget that there are many in the world who do not have sufficient to eat even for one day?

If we bear this in mind, we may well find this enables us to make an appropriate response to the needy, both through 'food banks' locally, and supporting world-wide charities as they look at the wider needs of the human race.

Lent is a time for us to reflect on our own inner spiritual needs, but when it comes to the crunch, we soon discover that the 'inner life' of faith cannot have real meaning without a wider concern for others. For we are 'members one of another', both in the fellowship of the church and as 'citizens of the world.'

May this thought be strong in our prayers at this time - especially we pray for Peace among all peoples.

March

Caught speeding

With a bit more order and structure slowly coming back into my life, I said to myself recently while out shopping, 'David, you're doing better than you think you are!'

When I arrived home, there was a police summons to say that I had been caught speeding in a notoriously common speed-trap area. I could either attend a special course or lose three points on my driving licence and pay a fine.

I've opted to go on the course!

It's the first time that I have been caught speeding in over 50 years of driving. I was rather upset but, as I shared the news of what had happened with other people, I soon discovered many others who had been caught in similar situations, even in the same place!

A fellow chaplain said to me, 'Congratulations, David, on joining the club, the biggest club in the country!'

When you share a concern about yourself with other people, how quickly you discover others who have had similar problems, but it is equally important that we listen to what other people have to say, especially lonely people, about the anxieties and frustrations that they face. How much they can benefit from sharing with us things that worry them. There is an old saying which says 'a trouble shared is a trouble halved', and it's true.

‘Lent’ is a time for ‘listening to what God has to say to us’, but sometimes we can discover much of what God wants us to do simply by listening to the needs of the needy and so share with them their burdens and concerns.

May ‘Lent’ make us all good ‘listening posts’ and positive in our actions for the Kingdom of God, as we listen to the concerns of those around us.

With all good wishes, and every blessing as we share in this time of self-examination together.

April

Visiting New Zealand

Last week I returned from New Zealand where my brother has lived for the last 40 years. My sister Esmée and I made the journey together, and it was the first time that I had visited my brother there, although he has been to see us a few times - even when we were in the Shetland Islands. There was a tremendous amount of reminiscing between the three of us - much of it covering more than 60 years!

We also saw much beautiful countryside, visited Maori townships, places of historic interest and enjoyed some warm weather. Returning home via Birmingham airport, the first thing I did was put my anorak on.

It has taken quite a few days to get back into things again, and I find myself and my family facing the first anniversary of Pauline's death on the 5th of April. As you can imagine the sense of loss is still strongly with us.

This year the fifth of April happens to be Easter Sunday. It is the day on which we celebrate the victory of Jesus over death. We must never forget this, and live with the joy and the positive attitude that the first Easter Day brought to the first disciples. It is for us to share in too.

A hymn of Brian Wren reads: 'Christ is alive! No longer bound to distant years in Palestine'.

The Easter message is one of hope for all. As we do our best to follow Jesus' example in all things, may we take the Spirit of the risen Christ with us into situations both of sorrow and of joy.

Easter blessings be yours.

A good breeze rapidly blows things dry

Monday is traditionally 'washday'. We might look upon it as a chore and a burden, but it does have some positive advantages. It gives shape to the first working day of the week and adds to the variety of things we do. It may well give exercise to muscles that do not get used in a computer-TV age as often as they should!

We need to remember that it doesn't necessarily have to be a nice day to get the quickest drying results. It can be bitterly cold for instance, but a good breeze rapidly blows things dry.

Life can be like that. We can have difficult days and times, but we don't always have to wait for perfect conditions to get on with the task in front of us. Just as St Paul says we must 'preach the word in season and out of season', so we must be prepared to do vital things that are pressing to be done at the earliest viable moment. To delay may mean they will never get done!

We all face dilemmas, but the question is: when we get clues given to us, even hunches that certain things need to be done, do we carefully follow the leading of The Spirit that leads us along this way? From a Christian point of view, we would say that 'we seek the guidance of the Holy Spirit.'

My hope is that we all learn how to be sensitive in taking on board all the factors that make for good decisions in our lives which are not just for our own benefit, but even more especially for the good and well-being of others.

June

Seeing things in a different light

Recently I've had new glasses, tinted varifocals which go darker in strong sunlight.

They take a bit of getting used to, but I am already finding the benefit. The older we are, it seems, the more often we need to have our eyes checked!

I find in this something of a parable. We always need to make adjustments and improvements in the way that we see things. It is part of lifelong learning and, unless we continually adjust our lives, we quickly become part of a time warp.

All kinds of things shape our outlook. Even the mistakes we make often help us to see things more clearly, and should help us, in the future to make judgements and decisions of a more mature kind.

When we look back on our lives, I'm sure that many of us squirm at the things we did; but hindsight can help us to see life more clearly through our failures and mistakes.

Wearing tinted varifocals makes me think of St Paul who says to the Corinthians, 'Now we see through a glass darkly, but then face-to-face'. These words are translated in various ways but they all lead to the same conclusion, that 'mature vision' is needed in order to face the realities of life. However, Paul also reminds us that there are only three eternal realities:

'Faith, Hope and Love, and the greatest of these is Love.'

My hope is that we will all be able to see that we need to be 'perfected in love.' In the end this matters most of all.

P.S. Anna came over especially to help with a garden party in our garden supported by local friends in aid of the Nottinghamshire Hospice and the Nottingham Maggie Centre.

July

Nibbling along

When people ask, 'How are you getting on?', my answer often is, 'I'm nibbling along fine thanks!'

It's a phrase I use to describe how I feel at the moment, in a time of great adjustment. The advice that people give us at such times is 'take a day at a time.' There is something biblically important about this advice too. Even in the Lord's prayer we are to pray 'give us this day our daily bread.' All of us need to remember daily our dependence upon God, and 'nibbling' implies taking things step by step, bit by bit, especially as we learn how to cope.

However, 'nibbling' also reminds me of guinea pigs, always nibbling!

Likening human beings to guinea pigs needs to be taken with a certain amount of caution. I do not like the idea of these creatures being used for experimental purposes, especially when used to test out cosmetics.

There is a sense in which our lives are to be used to 'test things out'. 'Nothing ventured, nothing gained,' so the saying goes. We can't just play safe all the time. There has to be an element of faith in all of us. Not all things we do will be successful, but at least we can learn a great deal from venturing out into the unknown, and frequently find great enrichment as a result of this.

Ventures in faith can help to make the world a better place, but they require us to learn how to boldly go out into the future, in order to find new openings and create peaceful bonds of friendship for humankind.

In the best sense of the word: are we prepared to pioneer in our lives and be 'guinea pigs'?

With all good wishes for the holiday season.

P.S. Over fifty local friends joined us for this mini garden party. The weather was kind and around £350 was raised towards the two cancer care centres.

August

Getting up - again and again!

Bailey Matthews aged eight, a lad with cerebral palsy, recently took part in a triathlon at Castle Howard. Accompanied by his father, many of us saw him on TV, cycling, swimming and then walking unaided except for his frame, as quickly as he could, to the finishing post.

As he nears the end of the course however he leaves his frame behind and starts running toward the final goal. He falls three times in the last few yards, but just shortly before the finishing line he gets on his feet again and crosses it. As he does so there is a wonderful of a sense of achievement on his face, and a great crowd of well-wishers are highly delighted to see him finish.

I'm sure that we are all deeply moved when we see people facing challenges like this, but we too can be involved facing challenges in our own lives. Not as spectacular perhaps as in this boy's case but certainly making demands on our persistence and perseverance. We often call it 'life's journey' or 'life's pilgrimage.' Let's face it, we too may often fail and fall. How important it is to get up again, and persevere.

We will make our journeys in many different ways, but for many of us there is a sense in which through prayer we may feel that God is accompanying us, almost like Bailey's father accompanied him along the way. Whatever form our 'spiritual support' may take, may all of us find a true sense of encouragement and support in the challenges that life presents to us.

September

Generosity towards strangers

An issue that is concerning as all at the present time is the migration of large numbers of people into Western Europe. Many feel that there is a great danger of losing our historic identities.

This kind of movement of people has gone on from time immemorial. In the Bible, we discover that the Jews themselves 'wandered in the wilderness for 40 years', before entering the promised land.'

As a result of this, in Jewish land laws, a great emphasis was put upon generosity towards those who were 'strangers in their midst.' In some places it is suggested that by giving hospitality to the stranger, in other words to the incomer, you are 'entertaining Angels unawares.'

So many of us are very fortunate. We haven't got a clue what persecution, oppression and poverty are all about.

One thing is certain. A country that accepts the distressed from other places, in the long run, is enriched by those who bring with them their talents, their gifts and their enthusiasm.

We all need enrichment from people who are very different from ourselves. This not only includes migrants, but the needy who have always been around us in our country as well.

In a strange sort of way, we discover that any act of generosity and hospitality opens doors, and makes our lives much larger. I am reminded of the words of Jesus where he says: 'whoever loses his life for my sake will find it.'

The circumstances under which Jesus uses these words was rather different, but at every stage in his Ministry he stressed the importance of generosity and love to all in need.

May the countries of Western Europe act responsibly and generously to those in such a desperate plight, and may this be our personal attitude too.

October

Modern Anxieties

'Anxiety' is a state, you could almost say a disease, that affects us all at some point in our lives.

It's amazing how even the smallest things can niggle and unsettle us, and how we can accept some very important decisions with a single nod. It is important however that we do not let anxieties get us down.

Modern day life puts a lot of pressure on us all that our ancestors never knew. The digital age for instance can submerge us, if we're not careful, with its massive information overload.

However, anxiety is not a new phenomenon. Jesus had a word for the anxious who lived in his day. 'Take no thought for tomorrow, what you shall eat, what you shall drink, or what to wear...... but seek first the kingdom of God..... and all these things will be added unto you.'

There is a message here for all of us who live in a consumer society. We all need to ask ourselves: do we seek to live by 'kingdom of God values' or by various forms of self- indulgence?

We all need to get our priorities right, and when we do this it is more than likely that many of our anxieties will be seen in their proper proportions.

We may well find afterwards that we have more time to say a prayer for those who are going through extremely anxious times, and support some cause that will alleviate their sufferings and anxieties.

November

'Misty patches' provide us with fruitful times of reflection

The second day of November was dull and misty. Most of Britain was enveloped in low cloud, and we couldn't see very far. Many airports were in pandemonium. Flights were cancelled or directed to other places.

November is the season of 'mists and mellow fruitfulness'. Brightly coloured leaves and berries have replaced many flowers. Although we are entering a darker season of the year, the autumn colours are still richly represented on the trees, giving us a great deal of pleasure; but foggy days can be a real problem. They limit our vision and make us travel more cautiously, and take, as it were, 'one step at a time.'

There are stages in our life-experience too when we cannot see the way forward clearly. Although we feel the need to have objectives that have long-term significance, we all have to learn the art of travelling at a speed that is appropriate to our circumstances.

However, if we learn to travel according to our visibility, it is amazing how much more we will be able to take in. Moving at the right speeds will enable us to see, for instance, more opportunities to relate well to those around us, and be 'fruitful people.'

St Paul reminds us that 'the fruits of The Spirit are love, joy, peace, patience, kindness, goodness, faithfulness, gentleness and self-control.' (Galatians 5:22).

Let us take heart. We may find that 'misty patches' that slow us up provide us with the most fruitful times in learning about things that matter most of all!

December

Simple hospitality provides happiness

The carol, 'Silent night,' in describing the Nativity scene reads, 'Mary and Joseph in stable bare, watch o'er the child beloved and fair.'

In the birth stories, recorded in St Matthew and St. Luke's gospels there are many fascinating details of the birth of Jesus, but apart from the visit of the three wise men who bring gifts of gold, frankincense and myrrh, from a human point of view, the background to the story is very down to earth and basic, and there is no hint of the splendour that would surround the birth of a child belonging to nobility or royal birth.

We have an innkeeper unable to provide hospitality to a woman expecting a baby, and when the child is born, a manger acts as a crib or cot. Such a lot seems makeshift and temporary. It is the shepherds watching over their flocks of sheep in the night who get the message - from an angel and not from the people thought to be of importance and significance.

But there is joy in the hearts of Mary and Joseph even in this basic simplicity. Before long the good news of Jesus' arrival brings joy to friends, relations, and others who have waited patiently for the coming of the Christ-child.

This raises the question: what brings happiness to human beings? Can the feel-good factor ever be measured in materialistic terms? It is very doubtful. This is not to justify in any way the fact that there is poverty, disease, and malnourishment which make many people's lives a misery. We must all strive for better conditions for everyone who lives in the world; but happiness and joy can be found where there is a common aim and sharing, alongside good loving relationships.

Christ's coming into the world, we believe, is about God's love coming into the world as well.

Whatever your outlook may be, may this be a season where good intentions towards all kinds of people become part of our daily living. This is the only way in which people of different outlooks can live peacefully together. May we all pray earnestly for peace at this time, and seek after real 'feel good' factors, where there is a real sharing out of wealth, and concern for the whole of mankind.

May this Christmas season bring Joy to all, and may the New Year bring fulfilment in those things that matter most!

Chapter 6: 2016

'Perseverance and Proactivity'

Bereavement is not only experienced by many as a sad time but a disorienting one. Often in times of transition we have to make an effort to get used to being on our own. For me it was, and still is, a time of exploring and making new friendships. Filling the gaps created by loss. Others are able to be more dependent on the support of their families and long-term friends.

It calls for a deeper understanding of friendship, and often mixing more with a great variety of people we come to know, people we become fond of, people that we like, and learning to understand people we find difficult. We need to listen carefully to the experiences others have faced along their journey.

For some people, seeking appropriate friendships in later years can easily create situations very similar to adolescent and early adult years of 'seeking out' and 'finding' someone whom they might be joined to in marriage, frequently this time for a much shorter partnership.

Unexpected elements of grief can stay for the rest of our years, especially where there has been a good relationship, a strong emotional 'glue.' This should not make us afraid however of strengthening the remainder of life with supportive friendships of many different kinds. For this we can be truly thankful. We can give help to many others who are in the same situation as ourselves. We can even find ourselves closer to some folk who have never known supportive friendship before.

God created a world in which men and women cannot exist in isolation. Not only for procreation, but for the enrichment of men and women in their social, cultural, and economic life. Reading between the lines in the New Testament we quickly discover that Jesus saw how important this was. Women as well as men had an important role to play even in discipleship days in helping to spread the good news that Jesus came to bring. If we do not accept partnerships of friendships across genders, we can seriously distort the message Jesus came to bring.

Life-long learning teaches us so much that is important about making new friendships and new senses of belonging to caring communities which includes all ages and all kinds of people. More often than not we have to learn a great deal more about what love and caring means in its widest, and fullest sense. This can help us and others tremendously as we travel along in the later years of our lives.

Toc H, a movement to which I belong, includes in the 'points of its compass' the aim 'to love widely'.

January

We need 'grit'

Here in England, it's been a hard sort of winter in a strange way, wet, damp and dismal, but not very cold. The weather forecasters say that 'gritters' might well be out on the roads soon for the first time this year, scattering a mix of salt and grit on the roads.

January is not an easy month in which to make resolutions. Festivities of the Christmas season leave most of us a little jaded, rather unwilling to get 'keyed up' for action. Sometimes we wish we had a better base from which to start. If only we had better skills, gifts and qualifications, more time and energy, how much more we might be able to do!

West Point, the training academy for aspiring army officers in the United States, is regarded by many as one of the most formidable educational institutions in the world. Candidates have a tough training, and the tests, plus other ingredients of talent, are likely to predict the success of those who apply.

However, 12 years ago a psychologist introduced what was called a 'grit' rating test. It consisted of 12 questions or statements, which expressed how much grit and determination the candidates possessed when facing difficulties. It has produced significant results.

Jesus described those who follow him as 'the salt of the earth' in other words 'gritty people' who are intent on doing what is right even in difficult and dangerous circumstances.

The question we have to ask ourselves is this. Is there enough grit in our make-up? Do we have the determination to persevere when things are difficult? Whatever resolutions we make at the beginning of the year will be useless If we do not have stickability. Jesus himself certainly possessed this quality. His 'grit', his perseverance, led to The Cross.

The challenges before us will not be as significant as what He faced, but let us pray that we may be people who possess 'gentle grit', so that we may accomplish good things that we intend to do - even if some of them might need to be adapted to changing situations.

May this New Year be one in which we make considerable progress in our good intentions!

February

Change may be hard work, but rewarding

Sometime soon, I shall have to do something that I'm not looking forward to doing. I will have to buy a new laptop computer, or at the very least move over to using a different system.

This is going to take quite a lot of getting used to, both in time, mental energy and a feeling of uncertainty as the process takes place, but it is something that just has to be done.

I have always been a great believer in lifelong learning. It is one of those things that I believe is a must for those who follow Jesus; but most of us like to learn new things that are a form of building on patterns and experiences we already follow. It comes as a shock when we have to undo things that we have done in a different way over many years. However, we are guaranteed that if we make these changes, we will benefit tremendously from them.

Life calls upon us to be bold when it is time to make changes. We are not far away from Lent - a time for personal reflection. During this time what are the things that we must change that will make us better equipped to serve God and humanity better than we've ever done before?

Change may be hard work. The challenge will be different for every one of us. If there are some areas where, it seems, we have to start all over again, may we be willing to accept the challenges.

March - Easter

If we rest, we are truly blest!

Life has to be kept in balance. If we try and do too much, we can easily upset the whole. Life is not a matter of working hard all the time. There used to be an old saying 'all work and no play makes Jack a dull boy.' However, overwork creates more than dullness. It is destructive and distorting. We all need rest times and a day of rest. The book of Genesis suggests that even God needs a day of rest too!

However, Sunday, a traditional religious and practical rest day, has another thought behind it. In the Christian setting it is known as the Day of Resurrection. This day of rest is known to us as the day when Christ is raised to everlasting life. On Easter Sunday, especially, worshippers sing 'Christ the Lord is risen today. Hallelujah!

None of us can work continually. If we try, we soon suffer from burnout which can easily lead to depression - even despair. We all need leisure activities, hobbies, and all kinds of things that we enjoy. They can all be included under the heading of rest, but they can also bring us to life again in the tasks that we are appointed to do.

May we all have a very happy Easter and enjoy some leisure time as well!

April

Inspiration from distractions

As predicted, the changeover to a new laptop and Windows 10 was not easy. It has been very slow work to get back to a routine again - hence the great delay in this letter.

Unexpected problems and distractions can be very wearing, and often create in us an anxious state of mind, but they often, even continually, remind us that life for us all has to be taken one day at a time.

When Jesus, in the Lord's prayer, says 'Give us this day our daily bread,' he is saying something more profound than asking God to give us food for our bodies to keep going, although that is a crucial meaning as well. These words are also reminding us that we need fresh resources every day to motivate us through the tasks that need to be done.

Sometimes however even distractions can be inspirational and help us along our way.

Although I'm not very fond of grey squirrels, this morning I found myself captivated by watching one building a drey high up in a tree in my garden. Seven or eight times it came down into the garden to collect more leaves and small sticks which it carried in his mouth. It dashed up one smaller tree and then jumped across to another, holding on to the slenderest of branches, but also holding on to the sticks and branches in his mouth, eventually reaching the rather untidy drey that was being built. Lots of determination, energy, skill, 'swingability', and accuracy were displayed in every one of his journeys.

We never know what kinds of things come along to inspire us, but we may see even in distractions examples which will help us to persevere with the tasks in front of us.

Faith and prayer go together

Recently I shared in a vigil which took place from midnight to 3 o'clock in the morning.

A neighbour, curious to know more, asked, 'What will you be remembering during that time?'

'Praying for the world in all its need' seemed to be the most appropriate answer.

A vigil of this kind is a tall order. We believe that 'prayer changes things' but our input is so small, it might even seem inconsequential in proportion to the vastness of human need.

Prayer in contemporary spirituality often has in mind 'the art of the possible,' and might go no further. This 'art' of 'mindfulness' and awareness of possibilities around us does have a very important role to play; but faith requires us to go further. Jesus in St Matthew's Gospel says, 'Truly I tell you, if you have faith as small as a mustard seed, you can say to this mountain, 'Move from here to there,' and it will move. Nothing will be impossible.'

I think he was speaking figuratively, but nevertheless making a profound point. Faith and prayer go together; and there are times when we are called to look beyond 'the art of the possible' and pray to see greater things happening.

'Praying for the world in all its need' may often seem frustratingly complicated, but we are nevertheless to keep it at the centre of our prayers - seeking harmony amongst all peoples so that we see glimpses of The Kingdom of justice and peace. This is surely something that all people of goodwill have in common.

May we give support to our leaders who seek solutions through diplomacy but may we pray for even deeper insights and compassion into the issues that need to be resolved, and live in the hope of their fulfilment.

Prayers@12 in the Summerhouse

June

A horse called Common Good

Last weekend, when travelling by train to North Wales, I found myself in a reserved seat sitting amongst a group of young men who had been university students together. They were on their way to a race meeting at Chester. Apparently, every half-year they meet up to spend a day at the races. They were full of enthusiasm, but in no way exclusive in their conversation.

They made me completely at home in their company. They offered me bottled beer, and salted peanuts. I politely declined the beer, and showed them a hip flask which I drew out of my pocket containing water. You can just imagine how they pulled my leg over that!

The person at my side was keen to tell me more about their work. They had trained as osteopaths, and were all keen about their profession. I learnt a great deal about how they operate and, quite incidentally, a great deal about the way in which the human body works as well.

As they were about to leave the train, one of them asked me what my profession was.

'A retired clergyman, a Methodist minister,' was my reply.

'Perhaps you might say a special word to 'the One Above' that we might back the right horses.' said one of them.

I replied that I would think about it!

I'm not a betting man, but I imagined myself going to a race course, and if there was a horse called 'Common Good 'I might be tempted to bet on it.

Seriously though, I do believe that in the forthcoming EU referendum, we need to bear in mind the 'common good.' We should be concerned about praying for a kingdom which has the concerns of all kinds of needy people at heart. How well off most of us really are.

July

Sowing seeds of hope

There are times when we can all feel 'under the weather.'

It might be created by the actual state of the weather; long periods of rain, coldness, or simply cloudy skies. I suspect that, as we get older, we are more easily affected in this way.

For others, it might be trends in national life, and contemporary political emphases which we feel are going in the wrong direction. Or it might be changes in personal health, relationships and circumstances. All these things and many others may make us feel low spirited, and lacking in motivation.

Prayer and our faith can help us along the way, and at some point, often do, but it is not always as simple as that. We often have to act positively even if we do not feel 'rock sure' of the direction in which we are going.

In difficult times it is important to plant 'seeds of hope'.

We may not always see the results of what we plant immediately, but we are called upon to go adventurously forward, believing that, as Paul reminds us in his letter to the Galatians, 'as we sow, so we will reap.'

At the Methodist conference held last week, those of us present were given a wristband to wear, with these words on it. ***'Do justice, love, kindness, walk humbly'*** with our God. These are words which we could well take to heart as we sow 'seeds of hope'.

Right attitudes of mind are so important for us all if we are to take an active, useful part in our communities, the world in which we live, and caring for our neighbours too.

August

'Beware of the barrenness of a busy life'

There is a famous saying attributed to John Wesley that says: 'Lord, may I not live to be useless.'

John Wesley was a very industrious person as well as being someone who stirred people into a genuine, healthy and enthusiastic sense of serving God in the world by encouraging them to follow Jesus, and serving their fellow men and women.

I think however it is also important to recognise that Wesley did not pray. 'May I always be busy!'

It is valuable, of course, that we do live our lives in as fruitful a way as possible; but just think of the consequences of being busy without giving any real thought to why we're busy!

There are times when we just have to take stock, rest, and reflect. The ancient philosopher Socrates once said, 'Beware of the barrenness of a busy life.'

Busy-ness can easily become a kind of ego trip. It can sometimes ruin other people's work. By our talking about what we can do, we can easily lose our sense of working as a team. Teamwork is extremely important in every kind of activity that is working for the common good.

I strongly believe that every one of us has some kind of calling in life. It may be a particular attitude that we possess in being able to do things quietly, and supporting others in doing their tasks. The role that we have to fulfil may not necessarily spring from a highly specialised professional role. Others may not even be aware of the particular calling that they have.

From a Christian point of view, from many other aspects of faith, and attempting to be fully human, we take on a 'servant role' which can give us a tremendous sense of freedom. When we discover what our real identity is, we will keep well clear of trying to be imitators of so-called successful people. What is important for us all is that we should be working out in our own unique way through prayer, meditation, and careful reflection, what our Creator wants us to be.

May we all discover what our 'useful role' really is alongside those pleasures and activities that we enjoy as leisure, and find fulfilment in them.

The way of discovery, I believe, is an ongoing process - from 'now unto eternity!'

Living a Holy Life

The Revd. Dr Roger Walton, who is this year's president of the Methodist Conference, has asked us as a church to consider the importance of living out a 'holy' life.

What does this really mean?

First of all, we have to remember what it doesn't mean!

It isn't about what we look like from 'the outside,' but what we are like from the inside. Jesus had some of his strongest words of condemnation against those who outwardly made a great show of religious observances, but inwardly they were full of deceit. He described such people as whited sepulchres!

Holiness is about becoming better people.

In order to improve, we have to take care that 'our left hand does not know what our right hand is doing.' In other words, we should do nothing for effect, but rather we should desire to do all things for the right reasons.

This is not easy. We cannot do it in isolation. John Wesley once said, 'The gospel of Christ knows of no religion, but social; no holiness but *social holiness'*. In order to become better people, we have to listen to and work with those round about us. From a Christian viewpoint we also have to be dependent upon the grace of God, learn from Holy Scripture, and the good examples of others.

Holiness, in practical terms for all of us, I believe, is about seeking integrity in our lives. It is an important ingredient for the well-being of society. May we all seek after holiness: it is an extremely important factor in making the world a far happier place, in which we play our part.

October

'if you don't use it, you lose it'

Today it has been announced that three British scientists have been awarded the Nobel Prize for their scientific discoveries.

How thankful we should be for all those make great scientific discoveries and add to our knowledge, as well as their own, especially where what they have learnt can be used to improve human conditions in the world and eradicate poverty, disease, and many other forms of ill-health. Knowledge is fascinating. The more we know, the more we realise what we do not know. It seems to be a case of what Scripture means when it says 'to the one who has, more will be given……'. The text of Scripture however goes on to say that 'to the one who has not, will be taken away even that which he has.'

On the face of it, this looks unfair. It looks like the conditions that the worst forms of capitalism create in the world, where the rich get richer and the poor get poorer.

But this isn't really what the Scripture is all about. It's more about diligence in using what we have, mentally, physically and socially. To keep on using all that we have for good purposes and the spiritual well-being of all is extremely important. It's more a case of Jesus, saying 'If you don't use it, you lose it.'

We are called upon to continually learn and develop: so much so that there is an eternal dimension to living. At the end we will see the value of this way of living.

'Good and faithful servant...... Enter into your reward.'

November

Real sages learn from younger generations

A book that I enjoyed reading earlier in my retirement studies, is titled 'From ageing to Sage-ing.' It is written by a Jewish rabbi, Zalman Schachter-Shalomi, and in it he 'gives ways to use our life experiences to nurture, heal, and perhaps save both the younger generation and this world.'

This ambitious book reminds us that in many former generations and civilisations, older people were valued for the wisdom that they could teach to the young. At the present time, there have been such rapid advances in science, technology, and particularly communication, that many older people feel that they have lost their role in society, and we need to recover ways of listening to what older people have to say.

This could be true, but one thing is certain: when older people start laying down the law as to how younger people should act, they are not listened to, and it soon becomes obvious that they have a lot to learn about present-day life themselves!

Last Christmas, my family bought me a 'tablet'. It's really great at sending and taking photographs, watching programmes on television that I've missed, and sending messages by email and such things as twitter, but there is one snag for many older people. If you have a problem in using it, who is going to help you to sort it out? It is more than likely to be a youngster who has been brought up in the computing age.

Scripture tells us that even 'out of the mouths of babes' as it were, wisdom and 'know how' can come. Jesus himself recognised that children have a very significant place in providing examples for older people of good living.

May all of us learn to be good 'sages', by remembering that we all have to continue learning, even especially, from those much younger than ourselves.

December

Hospitals and Christmas

This time last year, little did I expect that I would find myself just coming out of hospital after (another) cancer operation. Fortunately, all seems to have gone well; it's surprising what can be done with keyhole surgery!

The first thing that has hit me, has been the way medical teams carry out their extremely skilled tasks.

The work of the surgeons and doctors is central, but a whole team of people is necessary for success. The anaesthetists, the clerks who take great care in recording details, administrators, nursing teams, the assistants who weigh you, take your temperature, your pulse rate, and give the tablets you need, physio and speech therapists, dietitians, those who clean, dust and make beds, chaplains, volunteers who serve drinks, sell papers, direct visitors, Hospital visitors, relations and friends. All these roles and many others equally worthy of mention have real purpose. There are many who find great satisfaction and happiness in reaching out towards healing and wholeness for others.

Many today feel we are living in a sick world, and we all need to be sharing in a healing work that needs be done. Although our National Health Service is going through difficult days our hospitals provide inspiring models of how human beings should be working together in the world. Teamwork is needed everywhere where all kinds of people are genuinely valued.

As the Christmas season of goodwill approaches, team work for the common good needs to be embraced globally. For a true sense of good will is not possible unless we learn to work with others. May we all be willing to accept this challenge. This is what will make a really 'Happy Christmas.'

Chapter 7: 2017

Slowing up

Seamus Heaney in his poem 'Follower' reflects on how he admired his father. As a ploughman, his father would pick him up and carry him around when he was a small child, especially when he tripped and fell, but 'today it is my father who keeps stumbling behind me, and will not go away.'

In the earlier stages of life there is much stumbling, tripping and falling. It is all part of the growth of a human being, but in the later stages of activity, there is the weakening of muscles, changes in eyesight and hearing and many other factors contributing to the natural wind down of human life. These are things that we have to accept and be thankful that there was a time when we could do many things far more energetically, even tell others the things that we used to be able to do. We have a responsibility of course to keep ourselves as well as we can, and make sure that as far as possible we keep our faculties and abilities in trim. Many modern aids will help us along the way; but there is still a decline.

It isn't slowing up or slowing down that is our real problem. It is more likely to be the anxiety of whether we shall have time to do all the things we feel we ought to do and perhaps want to do. In our earlier years we express our personalities through the things that we do rather than simply 'being' the people that we are.

As we mature, we need to remember that 'slowing up' isn't about 'giving up' but rather taking gentle care with the details of good and compassionate living of every kind as we carry on our journey.

We also need to remember the words of Michel Quoist in his prayer 'Lord I have time.' We may not be able to do things as quickly as we would like, but spread over a longer period of time we can achieve more than we ever dreamt that we could. Aesop's fable of the tortoise and hare remind us of this. The one who travels the fastest doesn't always win. More time however needs to be spent on preparing what we think we ought to achieve. Real wisdom lies in learning the art of using our time in the right way. We must not let slowing 'up' get us 'down', but persevere.

January

In the New Year: 'Seek, and you will find'?

By nature, I tend to be an optimist, but there are some times when we all wonder how things are really going. My weeks leading up to Christmas were a bit like that. Two days before Christmas Day, I had to go for my check-up after my 'op'. The consultant was pleased to report that it had been completely successful, and that I was now able to drive again. All this news was a really good Christmas present!

When we are going through difficult days, many people remind us that attitudes of mind can have a great effect on how we feel. They will remind us of the need to get out and relate to people, to keep our interests going, accept any opportunities that come our way, and avoid situations where we may be tempted to brood on our own.

'Think positive,' is the advice given. And it's good advice; but it does it go far enough? Being positive requires that we do positive things, and not just think about them!

It is right that we should not habitually make rash and rushed decisions; but procrastination needs to be avoided too. We cannot stand idly by. Jesus says. 'Seek and you will find, knock and the door will be opened.' I believe that he meant this in a very practical way, as well as what you might describe as a 'spiritual' one. Whatever situation we are in, we should always be gently and even prayerfully exploring - seeking out information and support that will help us on our way, and in the process, help others as well. In this way, we will serve God in his world, our neighbours, and the whole of humanity in its wider needs.

Can I suggest that we adopt a simple motto for the New Year: 'Seek, and you will find.'?

We may not always find exactly what we think we need, but we may well find something better than we anticipated as we explore life, and its meaning. May we seek those things which bring about peace and contentment, think positively about the situations that we face, and ask for help for others in their decision-making too.

February

Keeping Serene

This week my central heating has not being working. Try as I may, I find the instructions difficult to follow. I await a visit from the gas engineer to explain things to me.

Technology often demands instant attention, and our own priorities get pushed on one side. Sometimes in computing we can achieve a lot very quickly, but it rarely leaves us without some new problems to face and new procedures to follow. If we fail to grasp the meaning of some important phrase in the instructions, we may find ourselves spending hours trying to do a simple task.

In the world, too there is always change. We feel great dangers in it at the present time because of movements and organisations with ruthless intentions. Issues of justice and tolerance call for our urgent attention and prayers. May the day quickly come when we can sail into calmer waters!

How do we stay calm when so many things are sent to try us? Do we feel harassed in our personal circumstances, or troubled by what is going on in the world?

The theologian Reinhold Niebuhr reminds us in a prayer that we should have 'the serenity to accept the things we cannot change, have courage to change the things that we can', and that we might have 'the wisdom to know the difference.'

However, even in the things that we cannot change personally, we must be willing to speak out in support of those who can.

March

We all need a 'tidying up' time

Ash Wednesday, yesterday, the beginning of Lent, was a significant day for me in an unexpected way. My home had a 'spring clean.' I do have some excellent help for a few hours on a fortnightly basis for many household chores, and this helps me along tremendously, but living on my own for the last three years has led to some areas of significant neglect on my part, and it's good to see the whole house looking in pristine condition.

In some ways, Lent is a bit like a spring clean. It is a time of year when we should set about doing some 'tidying up' in our lives, getting rid of excess baggage that has collected over the years, a sort of 'pruning down' process in order to help us live more wisely, efficiently and fruitfully.

There is a value in having some concrete objectives during Lent - some actual things that we do to improve our lifestyle in the best sense of the word. Giving up sweets, alcohol, smoking, rich fatty foods, even fasting may well help us to live much healthier, even longer lives; but there is always a much more fundamental question that we have to consider as Jesus did: what are we living for?

Basically, from a Christian point of view, we are called upon to 'to love the Lord our God' in every aspect of our lives, and to 'love our neighbours as ourselves.'

In other words, for all of us, whatever our outlook may be, we should be living for some worthwhile purpose. Our responses may be very different, but Lent presents a challenge to all.

May we make a good 'spring clean' in our lives at this time of the year, making sure that we do those things that matter most. This might include all kinds of unexpected things!

April

'Never grow tired of doing good'

Earlier this week. It was my privilege to take Holy Communion at two residential dementia care homes. We had been unable to take the service due to various members of the small team, including myself, needing hospital care. The last time we went was ten months ago.

After such a long absence. I felt quite nervous as to how everything would go but, apart from two minor hitches, all went well, and we all felt elated.

Because of our long absence I must admit that I had been wondering whether we should give up this kind of ministry, but the very fact of being there assured us that it was the right thing to carry on, and the residents who took part appreciated our visit.

However, it raises the question. 'When should we give up doing things?' Scripture says, 'never grow tired of doing good.' In other words, as long as we have cognitive skills to do things for others and with others, we should. Our 'old friend' John Wesley says 'do all the good you can... As long as ever you can.'

We may need to take more time to get things done as we get older (and even when we are not so old!), but perseverance is a quality we should never neglect but should cultivate at all times.

May the message of Easter inspire us to find new life, perseverance, and inspiration in the things that we do.

May

The simpler - the more we can share

Chuck Berry was a great inspiration to many musicians. The Beatles were greatly influenced by his style; but it was not just celebrities. Ordinary people became enthusiastic to make a 'joyful noise' as tunefully and cheerfully as they could!

In his early days, I was at College training for the Ministry. We had a skiffle group. I used to play 'the double bass'. It was made from an old tea chest and a broom handle with a cord tied to the top of the broom handle and the tea chest.

Although it was a very simple instrument, it was amazing how skilled you could get, and the notes produced had a distinctive quality about them. The improvisation required provided a challenge to us all, and money was scarce to buy quality instruments anyway. It wasn't an era that lasted for long, but we thoroughly enjoyed what we were doing at the time.

'Make a joyful noise unto the Lord' says the psalmist. When the Psalms were written many of the musical instruments were of a simpler kind, but they gave pleasure to those who worshipped God in this way and to human beings in their merrymaking too - even if the noise was not tuned to perfection!

We do not always have to have expensive equipment to entertain ourselves and others. Sometimes the simpler things are, the more others can join in.

Life does not just consist of the abundance of the things we have, but rather the good and proper use to which we put our possessions and our talents.

It is not easy to live a simpler lifestyle, but the challenge is there for us all. May we resist an overwhelming consumer style approach to life, and cut back more on those things which are not essential. Life gets cluttered so quickly with things that we do not need. In doing so, we would also be treasuring and valuing the world's resources so much more.

May we happily celebrate the month of May and enjoy many of the simpler things we take for granted.

June

'Love widely'

I recently sent out a tweet which said, '*We need to love widely'; to do this is 'to do justly, love, kindness, and walk humbly with your God.'* The first response (a 'like') to this twitter was from the president of our Methodist conference, another came from one of our police officers responsible for 'social cohesion' in a part of our city which is extremely multiracial. The officer is a member of a different faith from my own!

Learning how to 'love widely' is crucial in rapidly changing times. All of us are being challenged to move on from where we were in our thoughts and actions, not least about our national life. I believe that if we do not 'love widely' we rapidly become a backwater in the world.

'To love widely' however, does mean that we have to seek out justice in the world for everybody. We need to be compassionate and kind to all kinds of people, and learn how to *'walk humbly with our God'*. The person who first wrote these words was the Hebrew prophet Micah who lived several centuries before Christ, but he still has a very clear message for us today. Faiths are expressed in many different ways. How important it is that we walk humbly along the way we are convinced is the right way to follow.

We are facing many violent situations at the present time. Terrorism creates fear, but it can never put right anything that is evil in the world... But seeking the right things, and loving our neighbours as ourselves, in other words, being truly compassionate, kind and fair, is a surer way, and the only way eventually to bring about peace and happiness for all peoples.

P.S. Apologies for the long delay in sending this letter due to computer problems. At present the victims of terrorism and the terrible fire in the Grenfell Tower block are bound to be in our thoughts and prayers. We also remember those who are so valiantly helping.

July

Coping with the passage of time

Recently I was in St Albans to take the Church Anniversary at Marlborough Road Methodist Church, the last appointment I served in twenty years ago, before retiring as a Minister in pastoral charge of churches. It was good to meet again with a great number of friends in the congregation, many of whom I had not seen for a very long time.

I was wondering how I would get on. Whether I would recognise everyone, remember names, or whether they would think I looked and reacted very differently. To my great relief and delight, although at times, my response was rather slow, I remembered pretty well everyone there that knew me and there was a great sense of rapport.

I suspect that the older we are, time goes more quickly. Twenty years seemed only as if it were yesterday.

How do we cope with the passing of time? For some, reminiscing has a useful purpose. There is a value in being thankful for the past because it always has a lot to teach us; and it is rather interesting to note that a few people whom we may have found difficult to relate to in the past we now see in a different light. Ageing can often give us a deeper understanding and therefore a deeper sympathy with people who may have a very different outlook from our own.

We all have to learn how to value the past whatever age we are, as well as valuing the present. 'Living in hope' with a robust pro-active faith, explored gently and with compassion, I believe, is important. We all need to live with wider dimensions to our lives than just our own needs and discover 'eternal values.' This is what true religion is all about.

If we are to 'have life, and have it more abundantly' as Jesus said, we will need to put aside *some* time when we rest from our activities and consider what our lives are for. Even just a few minutes every day in prayer and reflection can make a great difference!

August

Neurological disorders

This morning when it was time to get up, I didn't feel like 'getting going' at all. I looked at my smartphone and found a message from a gerontological magazine which said 'don't forget to submit an article on neurological disorders!' I have never submitted an article to such a magazine but I felt in a strange sort of way it was saying something to me. Lack of motivation might well be described as a very common neurological disorder!

All kinds of factors in our lives can create a doldrums period, but then quite unexpectedly other things come along, sometimes other people, who play their part in helping us to make progress from our indecisive states of mind.

Needing to get on with my monthly letter, I suddenly felt that this early morning smartphone message was giving me inspiration. and my mind turned to St Paul's letter to the Romans where he says 'the righteous shall live by faith'. (Romans 1:17).

These words of St Paul have a strong religious significance; they remind Christians and others who believe in God that a person trying to live a good life has to live 'by faith.' Faith of many different kinds and in many different things is needed to give us the motivation to live out our lives in worthwhile directions.

All of us have days, when we have moments of uncertainty about the direction in which we should travel, but when it comes to the point, we have to take steps in faith. How important it is that we do.

May today be one of those days when we 'boldly go forward' or even 'timidly go forward.' May this happen frequently so that there may be a true sense of purposefulness in the things that we do. We might in the process well help motivate others to go forward in faith as well as ourselves.

September

A venture in faith

In less than a fortnight's time, we are trying out what for us is a new venture. Alongside the harvest festival, we are organising a 'FESTIVAL OF THE ARTS.' This is a project to open up our church buildings more to the community around us, and we are inviting people to bring along their paintings, drawings and other things that they have made to put on show for other people to see.

We need suitable panels on which to display works of art. We are also rather short of helpers and any offers of help will be greatly appreciated.

There is a sense in which this is a venture of faith which will take place at a time when we thank God for all that we have received, and pray for those who produce it. Needless to say, all the foodstuffs provided will go to people who need it. Will a Festival of the Arts work? Will people support it? We hope and pray that there will be a good response.

'Ventures in faith' however are not limited to things that go on in churches. In work, in good neighbourliness amongst all people we meet, and also in our personal lives we all have to make steps into the unknown. In these times of rapid change, we are called upon to trust in the unchanging nature of God. We all need an anchor to give us stability in uncertain times. We are not always successful at our first attempts at improving situations but we are given new insights I believe, into the way that we should go.

Life for us all is a challenge, and it simply withers away if we never do things that seem even just a little beyond us!

May we all be prepared to make responses to the challenges we face, and may we find blessings in every new and worthy venture we undertake.

Artwork by Jessica Boateng,
Student Exhibitor at Mapperley Art Festival

October

Like Topsy, it has 'just grown'

Like Topsy in 'Uncle Tom's Cabin', this monthly letter has 'just grown.'

It started off like a church pastoral letter, and mainly went to people in many different parts of the British Isles where I have served in ministry. Now it goes into many other walks of life even world-wide: friends of long-standing and more recent ones, people in leadership roles, in policing, church life, education, health and care homes, those who join in 'prayers @ 12' and also a very considerable number of friends who are having to get adjusted to living on their own.

Social media can give us a platform of our own choosing.

We must never think of it only being used by those who want to stir up strife and hatred in the world. Its easy availability does have its dangers, but it can be a tremendous force for creating a sense of community, cohesion, the Fellowship of like minds, and 'the common good.'

We need to express the truth as accurately as we can about life's issues. In St Matthew's Gospel, Jesus says that in situations when a lot depends on what you say; 'Let your yes be yes and your no be no!'. This is a tall order!

We can overload people with words. We suffer from information overload. Just a few well-chosen words are far more effective – making reading far more enjoyable and frequently more understandable.

Let us thank God for the many ways in which useful information and ideas can be conveyed to others today. They can be a means of giving pleasure to large numbers of people, and not simply as a 'tower of Babel' adding confusion and distress in the world.

Let us also pray that we will all use words wisely, sensitively, and for the building up of others in their needs as well as our own.

The Nottinghamshire Police Band at Southwell Minster prior to playing at the Emergency Services Carol Service

November

No two people's 'bests' are the same

We all have limitations.

Older people feel they do not have the capacity or the energy to do as much as they used to do and have to slow down. Others have disabilities and illnesses requiring lots of rest. Those who have limited incomes may feel unable to do the things they ought to do. Others in the heyday of their working experience may feel there are not enough hours in the day to do all that needs to be done.

We may have limits to the ways in which we help families and friends who live a distance away. Some have worrying and heavy workloads; the responsibilities of caring for others too may be onerous and without a break.

Limitations of all kinds can create a sense of despondency and stress. We all need 'faith' that helps us with these times, in addition to help we require from other sources.

We have to try and avoid anxiety, but also remember that no two people's 'bests' are the same. We are reminded of this in the true story that Jesus told.

When he was sitting opposite the temple treasury in Jerusalem, people were putting money into the treasury chest. Rich people were giving large amounts. Then there came a poor widow who dropped in two tiny coins together worth a penny. He called his disciples to him and said, 'Truly I tell you, this poor widow has given more than all the others. They had more than enough to live on, but she who has less than enough has given all that she had.'

In giving these two 'widow's mites' she was giving her best according to her means. We also have to remember that the limited amount that we can give is often of a far greater significance in our Creator's sight than we may imagine. We are all unique, we cannot compare what we are able to do with what others do.

My hope is that all of us will find contentment when we have done our best and when sometimes we feel it is very small, we must ask ourselves, who are we to judge its value?

Needless to say, we do need to examine ourselves and always seek to be doing our best. May we never tire of 'having a go.' If we venture in faith, somewhere along the line it is quite possible that we might come up with some pleasant surprises!

December (Advent)

'An unexamined life is not worth living'

During this last week I have been for a scan, a follow-up after surgery that I received this time last year. I suspect that we all get apprehensive when it comes to medical check-ups. There is a state of suspense while we wait for results which may take several weeks.

We all hope that the results will be good. Whatever is found is simply a report on what is there already! It still remains that we all tend to get rather nervous about any kind of examination, yet how valuable examinations are. The same is often true of educational examinations, although it does seem that some people have more natural ability in passing them!

Aristotle at his trial is reported to have said that 'the unexamined life is not worth living,' and I believe that this is true. In the Christian year, this season is known as Advent. Originally it was a period of self-examination before God so that we might be ready and better equipped for the coming of the kingdom of God which Jesus promises.

I also believe that times of examination are necessary for everybody, whatever their outlook may be. We all need to spend time looking carefully at the way that we live, that we may not be caught unawares. We all need times of testing, and none of us have a 'clean slate' as the saying goes; there is always something that can be done better. How disappointing it is when leading figures in society are 'caught out' because they have failed to respect important rules that are good and desirable for a truly healthy society. We all have to 'watch and pray' that we do not fall into temptation.

There is also a positive side to all this. After any kind of examination, we go forward with a clearer picture of what we need to do in our lives and will be better equipped to do it. I believe that every human being has a purpose, a 'calling' if you like, and we should all be aiming to fulfil it.

May we all spend some time carefully working out our calling - in whatever stage of life we are. It will be well worth our while to do this, and make us more useful in the tasks that lie before us.

With all Good Wishes for the Christmas Season, followed by a Happy and Peaceful New Year.

Mapperley Methodist Church,
closed October 2019

Chapter 8: 2018

Our calling

A special service called the Covenant Service usually takes place within the Methodist Church during January. It's a rallying call for us all to serve God well in the coming year.

Ministers wherever possible re-affirm their commitment at the yearly spring Synod for ministers, and frequently at the anniversary of their ordination as presbyters. At the Covenant Service we affirm our faithfulness together as a church to our own particular calling in discipleship, in following Jesus. All Christians should see their calling as a role to serve God in the world and to love our neighbour but e*very person in the world we believe is meant to have a role to play, a task to fulfil. We are all different: every individual is unique.*

Personal commitment to a task, or calling, can take place in many different forms and environments. My own ministry has had tremendous variety of experiences within it. For me, my style of ministry is undergoing a great test just now because the church which I have been attending and specifically helping in pastorally for the last twenty-three years as a supernumerary (retired!) Minister, has recently closed. There is a notice up at the moment that says 'for sale'. It's a great emotional shock. There are some who have been members for over 60 years, but all of us have to move on and find new ways of service and witness. There are times when we need to remember that we all have to be 'pruned' to be more fruitful.

Change though is always taking place and we must be willing to change the ways in which we express how we think and do things. If we allow ourselves to stagnate then we die. There is in the calling of all of us a challenge to respond, to move out of our comfort zones.

There is also the insight gained from seeing new 'doors' open, and new opportunities presenting themselves. May we be ready to follow The Spirit's guidance in all things.

While editing this anthology we have all been stunned by the Corona pandemic. The seventy-plus generation was requested to stay inside because of our "weaker immune systems." This disorientation affects us all. There is much heartache and sorrow, but much compassion and kindness are being shown too. People who are complete strangers are asking each other, "How are you?" when they meet in the street. As a schoolboy I remember the sense of togetherness we had during the war but I have never known such close community togetherness again until the present day. It is remarkably genuine. May it become a permanent feature for our future social life.

Times of transition create new ways of looking at life. This anthology began with a reminder that modern media can be used in very positive ways as well as negative ones. In this crisis we are entering more fully into the digital age. Even the telephone has far more extensive use. We can work, study, and keep in touch with friends, travel less and pollute the environment less.

Now, family members can't always be as close to each other at important moments in their lives as they would like to be. In this digital age it is possible to be linked together in vision and sound when loved ones are in hospital or for other reasons living far apart. We do look forward though to the day when we can hug again and be in each other's physical presence with a more profound understanding of what it fully means to be human beings, genuinely supportive of each other.

We need to take a worldview of our calling. We will not see all the answers to looking after our planet and its inhabitants quickly. In changing times there will be the need for more and more specialist tasks to be fulfilled, both humble and profound in their purpose. These are days which call upon us, whoever we are, to look at the issues that face us in a far greater way than we have ever done before. We will need to take up the challenge - individually and together.

'Open our minds Lord, that we may see the bigger picture.' ('Twitter' prayer, April 26th 2020)

January

'Come let us anew our journey pursue'

These opening words of a Charles Wesley hymn are deeply embedded in my mind. I was a teenager when I first sang these words, and they have come to mean a lot more since then.

Life is like a journey, and from a religious point of view life is often looked upon as a pilgrimage. At the beginning of a New Year it is a common experience to go through what has happened over the last 12 months, and we soon discover things that we didn't do very well. Sometimes we feel we did the very opposite of what we intended. We should be thankful and positive about all that, but it would be strange if we were happy with everything we did in the previous year!

It is a good thing for us all to give ourselves time for reflection, where we will learn how to 'think slowly' as Edward De Bono, the advocate of lateral thinking, would say. We are all people who need to take action to make the best out of our lives but at the same time carefully go through the issues that we have to face first, and we are all different. We cannot just copy anybody else, although good role models can certainly help us on our way.

It is a time of year when we ought to say 'we will make a new beginning, a new start', but it's quite a good idea to think carefully what the word 'anew' really means. It doesn't only mean 'making a fresh start' although that is important. It is also about allowing our lives to be filled up with new things that we require to continue progressively on life's journey.

All of us are called upon to treasure our lives and use them to the best of our ability. It is certainly essential to live according to our faith values; but all who desire to seek the 'greater good' will want to live life in the best way they can.

As we wish each other 'a happy New Year' and encourage each other on our journey, may we also express this as a desire or prayer which embraces the needs of others. May we give our New Year greetings to every kind of person around us - the stranger, the needy, both emotionally and materially - especially including those who have a very different life-style.

'Come let us anew our journey pursue!'

February

Kindness: A glue that holds us together

There was a fire recently at Nottingham station. I thought nothing about it until a fortnight afterwards I was travelling to North Wales for a family funeral. There was still considerable inconvenience. Lifts were out of action or difficult to find, and it was not easy to see directions to the platforms where one needed to go. For senior citizens it was necessary to carry cases downstairs to the platforms, and there were many passengers with anxious looks on their faces, hoping that they would get to their trains in time.

It was discovered that the fire was arson. What a lot of havoc that people with evil intentions of this kind and other forms of maladjusted personality, can cause.

But recently, at the other end of the county in the Mansfield area an experience of a very different kind took place. A 93-year-old was robbed. A Police Community Support Officer was sent to see how he was getting on. Discovering that the elderly gentleman was fond of music, the police officer sat down at his piano, and played one of Chopin's Nocturnes for him. It made the pensioner's day and the story of the pleasure it gave him went viral.

Human beings are capable of doing very destructive things on one hand and showing kind gestures on the other. We should never forget this, and certainly aim to show gestures of kindness to all kinds of people. Evil actions can create great havoc, but on the other hand we never know the extent that any gesture of goodwill or concern can have too.

We also have to remember that any religious or secular belief that doesn't have the element of kindness in it, is seriously deficient. Kindness in any form of concern for others is a glue that ultimately holds society together. It is up to us all to practise kindness wherever we can.

March

We all need support

Just now the roads and pavements here are very slippery. A doctor friend said to me, 'You ought to get a stick. As you get older it is so easy to fall. A stick is like another leg. It makes it so much easier to keep your balance.'

I have resisted having a stick for a long time mainly one suspects for vain reasons. We don't like people to think that we're getting old, but someone recently gave me a stick. It's appropriate to my height, and two days ago, rather self-consciously, I went out using it for the first time especially on a slippery day.

Straightaway I felt the benefits.

As human beings we can all act stupidly, and not use the extra help we need. Sometimes we underestimate our abilities to do things, but at other times we think we can go on as we have always done, failing to adjust to changing circumstances, and sometimes stubbornly refusing to accept help and advice that we are given.

We all need support in many aspects of our lives whatever age we are, and whatever our abilities may be. We may need the support of friends, spiritual support, the organisations to which we belong, our families, medical care and the facilities our local authorities provide. Likewise, we will want to give support to others; but there is something else I believe we need deep down in our being.

My mind goes back to the 23rd Psalm, where the Psalmist says, 'The Lord is my Shepherd, I shall not want'... And even in the darkest moments of the shadow of death he says, 'I will fear no evil, for you are with me, your rod and your staff they comfort me.'

The Psalmist puts his trust in God as the One who was supporting him - spiritually helping him along his way through life's struggles and anxieties.

We all need support, and often we have the privilege of helping others in their needs, but there is also the way of faith to which we are all invited to find another kind of support, and in our better moments, many of us try our best to follow.

We could well imagine the words of the psalmist when speaking of God's help and support saying, 'Your staff acts as my walking stick, and helps me along life's way.'

It's a thought that might help many of us, especially in our times of special need!

Our part in helping the lonely

An elderly person waiting for a bus said to me recently, 'I can't spend all day sitting in my house on my own with nobody to talk to.'

He then told me that he was going into Nottingham to the Victoria shopping centre where it is warm, some comfortable seating is available, and there's chance to chat with other people.

Loneliness can be very hard to cope with. The strange thing is that the more inhabitants there are in a town or city the easier it is to feel lonely. Wanting to 'get out of the house' is common amongst those who have been bereaved and often, the longer they have been together, the more intense their loneliness. Many do not live near their families due to their work, and neighbours may be out working all day.

We may be fortunate and have good neighbours who keep an eye on us, and help when needed. They are 'worth their weight in gold' as the saying goes.

Speech is a God given gift. Sometimes we can say too much and bore people, but we can all have a role where we are proactive in meeting the needs of others by sharing conversations with them, and an important part of that role is simply listening. Even just saying 'good morning' can sometimes be a splendid opening for conversation. It can make others feel wanted and, as we get to know people, we may be able to invite them in our homes to have coffee or more. What a great role shop assistants can have chatting while serving their customers. Likewise, medical staff while meeting the needs of their patients, and all caring professions.

We can all play our part in the battle against loneliness. We can help to make others feel unique simply by a few words of encouragement. Sometimes we do need to be on our own in order to think quietly, carefully and prayerfully; but basically human beings are social creatures, and even if they are suffering from illnesses preventing them from talking rationally or not even at all, they all need words from other human beings to help them along their way.

We are now in the season of Easter where Christians proclaim the message that Christ is 'alive.' Part of the Easter message is that in moments of loneliness we can be aware of 'another' who is travelling along with us on life's journey and beyond. Human company means a lot, but there is a sense in which the risen Christ waits to be our spiritual companion on the whole of our pilgrimage.

Prayer can help us tremendously. May we play our part in helping the lonely.

May

Lessons from 'Empire Windrush' days

My First Appointment as a Probationer Minister was in Coventry when large numbers of immigrants came from the West Indies via SS Empire Windrush.

They came full of enthusiasm, inspired strangely enough by posters in the West Indies with Enoch Powell's face on it encouraging them as citizens of the Commonwealth to help us in this country in our time of need.

It was an opportunity they keenly seized, full of excitement. Some brought their guitars and they would gladly strike up a calypso tune to entertain anywhere.

They took on many menial jobs. Provision had not been made for housing them. Rachman-ism exploited them terribly, and in looking around for accommodation they found notices saying 'no Blacks, Irish or dog owners'. A few were even exploited by their own islanders. In our local church we set up a 'West Indian Welfare Association'.

Unfortunately, there were churches who failed miserably in looking after their new worshippers who came from very different cultural situations, and many new kinds of churches arose as the result of situations of neglect. However, many did support their traditional churches in spite of the insularity in some instances that they had to face.

In my last appointment in St Albans I had the privilege of ministering to considerable numbers of West Indians again, spending a sabbatical in St.

Vincent and St. Kitts and, over most of the years of my ministry, baptising, marrying, conducting funeral services, receiving many into the membership of our churches and ministering to their spiritual needs.

How much Pauline and I valued, and I still value, the friendship of Afro-Caribbean friends, incomers from African countries, other parts of the world, as well as people from other parts of the British Isles.

My prayer just now is that all things that are designed to bring about social cohesion should be encouraged, the dignity of all peoples respected, and no one treated shabbily. The thoughts and aspirations of John Wesley also come to my mind. He considered that 'The Whole World was His Parish.'

June

Royalty, football and the created world

There are many vital world issues that need our prayers, and we must not neglect them, but three things have especially caught my attention during the last month.

The first is to do with royalty. I do not often follow their day-to-day activities; but the marriage of Prince Harry and Megan, now the Duchess of Sussex, illustrates the wider ways in which love can cross all kinds of barriers - racial, cultural and circumstantial. Their wedding, seen by many millions on TV, shows how much royalty have moved away from conventional restrictions on the choice of partners. We all pray that their bonds of marriage may be strong, and help them to be an encouragement to many people. We are already appreciatively aware of their concerns on social issues here in Nottingham.

Secondly, John Motson, 'Motty', has retired after 50 years as a football commentator. His enthusiastic commentaries have been a great source of entertainment to millions of people. I had the privilege of being his minister in St Albans. It is not commonly known that his father was a Methodist minister. He preached his last sermon on a harvest festival Sunday in my church and John read the lesson. John's commentating on football is going to be greatly missed.

Thirdly, after a rather cold and very wet spring there is an abundance of colour in the created world around us. Because of the weather many plants have set their own agenda and there is a profusion of life in our gardens and in the countryside around us.

This profusion acts as a reminder to us to take care of and understand more deeply, the ecology of the created world. Worldwide we must work for the common good. Not only does this mean caring for the natural world together, but also coming to a deeper understanding of how people throughout the world can live together.

It is good to know that Patriarch Bartholomew the First, the 'green patriarch', known by many as the leading patriarch of the Orthodox Churches, has taken up the cause of 'caring for creation' with great enthusiasm.

My hope is that all Christians, together with people of all faiths and outlooks, will take this issue seriously, and pray that we may look after all the good things that God has given us in the world.

July

What's in a Name?

Waiting to see your name appear on the screen in a doctor's waiting room can be a daunting experience but also an intriguing one. Many names, both surnames and forenames, may be strange to us, often reflecting the age, and their ancestral nationality. We might also ask ourselves the question, 'I wonder how a person with that name came to live here?'

Some names originate from various parts of the British Isles, but the scope now however is worldwide. How intriguing this is. Some might even find it frightening.

Whilst visiting my surgery recently, a rather unusual European name came up on the screen. To my surprise a woman I know quite well responded. I often have a chat with her. She lives nearby. I have always known her by her first name, but never known her surname.

It made me start to think quite differently about all the unusual names I had seen that morning. When we know people personally what a difference it makes!

Although there are sometimes difficult and puzzling issues we have to face when people come to live amongst us from other parts of the world, the hand of friendship and getting to know them as people and taking an interest in their welfare can make a tremendous difference to us all.

We all have a responsibility to create strong community life. It must be a two-way process of course but we all have a part to play in it. Good strong cultures are created by inclusiveness, and as Jesus would remind us from the Commandments and the story of the good Samaritan, 'You shall love your neighbour AS yourself.'

Are we prepared to live up to this great ideal? The well-being of the world depends on this.

People with dementia need friends

Quite often I lunch at several dementia care homes where I serve as a chaplain. This is very convenient, for whilst being on one's own, I do not have to get so many meals myself. I have been invited by the staff to go and have lunch with the residents regularly. This has been a very rewarding experience as well as a convenient one.

One must bear in mind that many residents in these homes do not get many visitors. Even those that have often possess very little verbal ability. Although they are in a rather confused state of mind, they are pleased to have someone sitting at the same table as themselves who is not a resident. The conversations, brief and confusing as they often are, usually have some grain of thought on which one can build a basic conversation. Even just a bit of communication can make their day.

There is another factor however that is very important in these visits. It is the role of the caring staff who have so many things to do as they look after the needs of the residents. The hot weather of this summer season has been particularly stressful for these carers who do such wonderful work. To look after people with dementia makes considerable demands on the inner resilience of these carers. Many of them do it as a calling in life, although they would not describe their role in this way.

I have found myself really enriched by visiting these homes by both residents and the caring staff. There is a real challenge in these situations for people to go in and spend time with those who need our support and interest whether they are related to residents or not. Many need friendship. They miss the wider contact with human beings. The question is 'Are we able to sharpen their quality of life by our interest and support?'

This letter may possibly need a response from someone who is reading it – a relative or a friend. Even a visit regularly for a few moments might surprise us by how effective it can be, but we may also find that some residents have patches of memory which are far sharper than our own!

September

Hot weather doesn't always help!

This summer we've had some wonderful weather. Long periods of hot sunshine and very little rain, but many people have found the weather rather trying. Most of us obeyed instructions and kept watering gardens to a minimum. The result was that lawns went very brown, in parts looking completely dead. Many wondered whether they would ever come back to life again.

Then after a long delay it started to rain. Now my lawn is back to three quarters of its natural greenness although it still has some way to go.

The exceptionally warm weather earlier in August brought to light some problems that are very common in society today - frequently summed up as part of the 'blame culture'. Intensely warm conditions have tended to make dementia care patients for instance, particularly restless and requiring more help. When there happens to be more than one person requiring help at a time, caring staff cannot be in two places at once; and if there is some mishap or serious problem arising, how quickly blame can be attached to harassed workers without the complete picture being seen.

Doctors, nurses and medical staff, police officers, teachers, social workers and all the caring professions have similar problems. Mentally, physically and emotionally workers can easily become exhausted with their tasks and sometimes even dread having to face up to what lies in front of them because there is too much to cope with at a time.

There are situations of course where there is neglect, but it can be due to the fact that people feel discouraged by the difficulties that they have to face. Jesus said, 'Judge not that you be not judged' and he reminds us that, as we judge other people, we will be judged ourselves because many judgements have not looked fairly at the whole picture that is faced by those caring for others.

We all have to be extremely careful in any assessment that we make in any situation. There is always a tremendous amount that we do not know. I believe that we all have a ministry towards other people, and it is basically a ministry of encouragement.

Society will be a much happier place when we replace a 'blame culture' with an 'encouragement culture!'

Let us remember in our prayers at this time all who are under great pressure because of their work as well as those who need all the care they can get. Carers need as much support as those who they are caring for.

October

Let's replace 'blame culture' with 'encouragement culture'

Many people are beginning to say, 'Let's replace the 'blame culture' with an 'encouragement culture.'

A blame culture is often negative and destructive. Innocent and often hard-pressed people become very unhappy when society criticises them when they are not really to blame.

An 'encouragement culture' is proactive - not just saying nothing evil but actively thinking and saying things that are good and encouraging to others, especially that they may explore new things for themselves. There is so much good advice in the words of Scripture that say, ‘Do not be overcome by evil, but overcome evil with good.’

Culture starts in our earliest days. Good culture starts in families, I believe, by teaching children to say ‘thank you’ to those around them, but it has to go out into every avenue of life, and every part of the world. We are never too old to learn to say thank you. Thankfulness and gratitude are deeply embedded in the culture of encouragement. Where these virtues exist, and we allow them to be firmly embedded in our personalities, it is likely that we may well become happier people in ourselves

At this time of the year in the Western world there are still many who celebrate harvest time when we thank God for the harvest, but alongside the fact that we always need to remember the needy, we also say thank you to the millions of people who have been responsible for the way in which our daily supplies of food have been met. It is an extremely good practice.

A blame culture fails to recognise the simple fact that human beings are human, and when under pressure especially can fall short of the best that they would like to do and be. As we encourage others, we also find the true meaning of community for everybody, for we all need to be 'lifted up 'in the environment in which we live.

May all of us become sensitive to the ways in which we can help build an encouragement culture. We all have a part to play in it. It can be infectious and grow. We can all feel emotionally healthier as a result. The older we are the more we ought to show gratitude and thankfulness when we receive it.

We also need to discover ways in which we can help in the well-being of all around us. creating positive attitudes of encouragement. It is something that can become reciprocal.

November

May we learn from history

The first time I went to Berlin was during the Cold War in 1955. I travelled in the 'Berlin corridor' at night and I only saw the inside of a very overcrowded train.

This October, 63 years later I saw a vibrant city. The first night we went on a short river cruise and viewed many of the historic buildings of Berlin. On the second day we travelled on a sightseeing bus. We were told that 70% of Berlin was destroyed during the war, but as a result, many unique and imaginative buildings have been built.

World tourists were there in large numbers, and much that we saw was very emotional: remains of the Berlin Wall, individual memorials to men and women who had tried to swim across the River Spree to escape from East Germany, only to be shot in the process, the Holocaust Memorial, a memory garden to Jews and Romanies who had been murdered during the Nazi regime. Near remains of the Berlin Wall was a photographic display of politicians, creative thinkers, Jews, gypsies, disabled people and those classed as imbeciles who 'stood in the way' of a programme of ethnic cleansing. A sober reminder of what can happen in any part of the world when democracy gets seriously damaged by oppressive populist leaders.

This regime began amongst those who perpetrated hate crimes and threatened all who resisted their policies. Great bravery was needed to stand up to these pressures by anyone who wanted to see 'right prevail.'

The day on which I started to compile this letter is known in the Christian calendar as 'All Saints Day' when we remember all kinds of people who have stood up for what is right, and sometimes had to pay heavily for the consequences. 'Blessed are the peacemakers' says Jesus in the Beatitudes, 'for they shall be called the sons of God.'

Let us at this remember all people who have shown great bravery, and suffered much when true law and order in society are being damaged, especially this year as we remember the centenary of the ending of the First World War.

It is important however that we all learn the art of speaking the truth in the face of evil in the world. May we all be willing to follow the good examples of all those who have gone before us.

Processing to War Memorial at Nottinghamshire Police HQ

December

The value of friends

In an article I read recently, I came across these words: 'We can never underestimate the value of friends.' This I believe is important at every level of society and in many different kinds of friendships - some lifelong and others that sometimes drift in and out of our life experience.

Never has there been a greater need for human beings to develop the gifts of friendship, they are gifts which will serve us well throughout our lives. Those of us who have lost our partners or people who are desperately lonely for any other reason find many friends a source of great blessing, and we can all reciprocate by listening to what their needs are. It requires trust, and a willingness on our part to really listen.

One of the most fascinating and helpful things that can happen to any of us is to have a conversation on a train, bus or plane where we find ourselves talking with someone we have never met before and are unlikely to meet again. This happened to me recently on a long train journey where a woman shared with me her life story of relationships, and how she was hoping that in the future she would meet someone with whom she would build up a permanent relationship.

She wanted to hear what my story was, and I related to her my own sense of loss, and how I had been helped tremendously by a great variety of friends. It was a great experience of friendship between two strangers who enriched each other.

In many ways for me the experience of bereavement has helped my understanding of other people's sense of loss and in a strange way it has enriched my pastoral ministry.

As we celebrate Christmas, whatever our outlook may be, can I suggest we especially give thanks for our friends. It may be appropriate to do this in our prayers, or even add the name of others whom we ought to befriend especially because of their special needs.

The Christmas season of Goodwill is also the season of Good Intentions towards every kind of person. This was the message of the Angels on the first Christmas Day, that there should be peace on earth. We should have an attitude of friendship towards all people we meet, perhaps especially in political situations where it is very easy for attitudes of hatred and ill will to flourish.

Let us pray for a CULTURE OF FRIENDSHIP to be strengthened throughout this Christmas season and be thankful to God for all who have shown us friendship and support in our times of need.

Chapter 9: 2019

Travelling on the right lines

Recently, one of my tweets read, 'May our minds be prized open to receive new insights into our understanding of life and make a good response to what we learn.' Insights do need to be gathered from every part of everyday life. Ultimately, I believe they are all God-given. May we all continue to travel along this way....

We all need to review where we are on life's journey. We may experience moments when the bottom falls out of our lives – when we lack stability and helpfulness because our circumstances have drastically changed. The future can be frighteningly nerve racking, but at the same time movingly challenging.

Slowly, new horizons appear; new openings for service, often very different from what we have done before We have to go out and explore. The true life of a church for instance is never just centred around a building. A verse of Scripture reminds us that we have 'a building from God, not made with hands, eternal in the heavens.' There is a continuing search for life and meaning, with changing forms and patterns. We understand God working in different ways according to the age in which we live, but we must simply trust in God wholeheartedly to lead us on. We travel on by faith.

A group of us who were students together at Didsbury College in Bristol have met together twice yearly for many years at Mount St. Bernard's Monastery in Leicestershire. We often remember the principal of our college, in the middle of the 20th century, saying to us that 'faith is faith.' These three words still ring true. We can be in a state of mind however like that of the father whose son is healed by Jesus. He cried out before the healing took place, 'I do have faith but not enough. Help me to have more!'. (St Mark, 9:24)

I was asked recently by a good friend the question 'do you ever have doubts?' The answer is 'yes', and sometimes there is a struggle to see the way through; but what we also have to remember is that doubt can sometimes play an extremely important part in helping our faith to grow. We may have an experience described by St John of the Cross as 'the dark night of the soul.' Even Jesus himself at times was severely tried and tempted.

We see this in his temptations in the wilderness, in his cries of agony on the Cross. We see it on many occasions with the disciples, especially with the disciple Thomas who doubts the reality of Christ's presence with them after his resurrection. The reply of Jesus includes the words, 'How happy are those who believe without seeing me.' (John, 20:29)

We can be like the father whose son needed healing. We too may need to confess that we do have a bit of faith but not much.

'Lord help us to have more!'

Mount St Bernard's Monastery, Leicestershire

January

Hobbies and progress

A model making shop in Nottingham is closing down, not due to lack of trade, but simply changed circumstances. It has been very busy over the last few weeks, especially with model train enthusiasts who have found all kinds of bargains as a result of the clearance sale.

Many of the customers are middle-aged and older men for whom model railways is a fascinating hobby. It's all tied up with the earlier age of steam, trainspotting, steam locomotives thundering through our local stations, and the excitement of a steam train taking some of us on our holidays.

Steam locomotives are to be found in railway museums, and many men especially give a great deal of their leisure time in restoring them, and yet others enjoy being engine drivers for preservation railways, and fulfilling other roles.

The age of steam also reminds many of us of a time when it was still a way for people to travel out of their local communities and explore new ground. Cars, coaches, aircraft and holiday cruises have taken over much of this role since.

Model steam railway engines and preservation societies have created a healthy kind of looking back, but there are many other forms of looking back that are simply a kind of nostalgia where there is an unwillingness to change. Such attitudes can have a negative effect on our personalities.

My prayer is that we may all appreciate things from the past, live in the present and move forward into the future, because life is like a journey or even a pilgrimage where we have to move on, striving to achieve good objectives with a good end in view. Sydney Carter's hymn, 'One more step along the world I go,' reminds us of this when he writes, 'It's from the Old I travel to the New, keep me travelling along with You.'

We all need to keep on moving and preparing for new experiences whatever age we may be.

My wish is that 2019 may be a progressive and happy year for us all.

Look where you are going

As we get older it is surprising how things our parents said to us as children come back into our minds. One came into my mind today. 'Look where you are going.'

We need to look where we are going, both in the things that we are doing and in the things that we are facing. Our lives all need a sense of watchfulness about them. Never has there been a greater need for people to pray and to think carefully about how we are living, how we are affecting each other, and how we are looking after the world and its resources. We need to keep our eyes open to all these issues.

We must look beyond fake news and destructive hidden agendas; but we must also look out for signs of positively good things happening in the world and encourage them to grow.

When Jesus tells us to pray, 'Give us this day our daily bread,' we are not only to make a request for nutritional body support, but for all the other things that enable us to exist, accepting each day's 'diet' as it comes, 'watching where we are going,' and accepting the good things thankfully that we are given as we travel along life's journey.

We can easily be overcome by the negatives presented to us, but each day also has opportunities to enable us to live together better than we've ever done before. We must remember that there is The Spirit at work in the world too, waiting to show humankind the way to abundant life.

In John Bunyan's hymn written in the 17th century entitled, 'Who would true valour see', there are some words which seem appropriate to the age in which we live. He writes:

'Who so beset him round with dismal stories,

do but themselves confound; his strength the more is.

No lion can him fright; he'll with a giant fight;

but he will have a right to be a pilgrim.'

Let us all 'watch where we are going', and go

forward, challenging the inferior things that go on and accepting all the good things that we are given to share with others in faith - a day at a time and travelling in the right direction.

March

Is any journey ever wasted?

Recently I went to visit a friend in hospital but when I got there the ward was closed because of infection. It seemed a wasted journey; but I think the truth of the matter is that no journey need ever be a wasted journey. There is always some thought to think about that fills the gap, and what appears wasted time allows other things to come into our minds that help us to see more clearly what life is all about.

We can spend time on a journey simply observing people. Three quarters of the travellers on the bus, train or tram may be dipping into their smart phones. There is the endless excited chatter of children and, more in the centre of a city, many different languages. We begin to realise how cosmopolitan we are. We might meet up with someone we haven't seen for ages; but there is another side that is equally important.

The journey can be a very creative one. Just now we remember Lent. How important the time was that Jesus spent in the wilderness. Barren and wasteful 'wilderness' times can be times of reflection, contemplation, and prayer. The opportunity to do this is in what one writer in his Lent book described as 'times of leanness.'

For Jesus, Lent was a time of preparing for ministry, of spreading the 'good news of the kingdom of God.' This kingdom has qualities of gentleness and not violence. However we understand life, I believe all people of goodwill need to be working for the common good. There is no doubt in my mind that Jesus saw the importance of all people in the world who work for justice, 'righteousness' and peace.

We all need to remember that peace in the world is not just the absence of war but a time when justice, fairness, compassion, forgiveness and goodwill are predominant both in world affairs and in the lives of individuals. We are all called upon to be peacemakers.

Surely this is something for all to work towards during Lent?

May we all spend time in thoughtfulness during this season so that we may all be better equipped to serve each other and to serve God in the world.

April

We are all on a journey even if we cannot travel

Recently I met two neighbours who were just going out for a walk round the local park. It was a nice sunny day, and good to see the arrival of spring. They were looking forward to their stroll.

Many people are not able to get out, mix with other people and enjoy stimulating things outside. However, whether we are 'home' bound or not, we are all on a journey which is shaped by our experiences along the way of life. Even if we are not strong physically, we are mentally involved in travelling but journeys are not always easy.

The Jews under Moses spent 40 years journeying in the wilderness going through hard and unsettled times in order to find a better place to live. We are reminded of this in the hymn, 'Guide me, O thou great Jehovah, pilgrim through this barren land.'

At present as a country we are going through a journey of political uncertainty too. Our prayer is that as a country and as individuals we will work for things that will be for the good of all - world wide as well as locally and as well as in our own experiences of life.

The big question however that faces us, both as a nation and as individuals is this: are we able to journey through life with faith, hope and love in our hearts? Whilst there are not simple answers to life's questions, it is a tremendous help if we can believe that underneath all life's difficulties there is a faith by which we can live. St Paul saw the importance of this and said that 'there are three things that last for ever – faith. hope and love, and the greatest of these is love', and love is at the centre of the first commandment which is the greatest of them all - to love God and our neighbours as ourselves.

May all 'barren' areas of our lives and in society be blessed during this period of Lent by new insights that will help us all on our journey.

May

De-clutter but still sow seeds

Since recent property repairs, much in my outhouse had to be cleared out and thrown away. A skip load of things no longer needed had to go. Many items had been kept over 20 years, things that might be useful 'sometime.'

I decided however to keep some unused packets of seeds. Although some are several years old, I discovered that the seeds were double packed in foil so that many could still be planted.

We all need to de-clutter. Sometimes simply so that we can find things we are looking for, but we also need to de-clutter our minds too. All of us carry 'baggage'- attitudes, prejudices, dislikes and many other things that hinder us from being the kind of people that we really ought to be; but there are some qualities and attitudes that we ought to keep. They are like seeds that have been packed away tightly and securely for a very long time, and they still need the opportunity to develop, grow and be fruitful. The 'seeds' of our personalities have to be cultivated, and even if some of these seeds or traits of personality have not been brought into play for a long time, they can still occupy a very significant place in our lives.

We need to explore, and at whatever age we are, set seeds for the future. They may not all be for our benefit, perhaps for future generations, but we must always be purposeful in our living and at the very least sowing seeds for situations beyond our own. This includes caring for the natural world as well as what we might describe as the spiritual and the social needs of others.

We should all concentrate on planting seeds, that others as well as ourselves may benefit from and enjoy abundant life. We should plant seeds that give encouragement to others and help them to grow and mature.

May we all prosper by sowing seeds of hope - through our giving, through generosity of spirit, and through our prayers.

June

Varieties of loneliness

What surprises me is how many different forms loneliness can take. Here are just a few.

There is the loneliness of those that have no friends because they find it very difficult to make friends. For some, things have happened which make them very nervous and not able to trust in others to build long-term relationships again. Others have lost loved ones through bereavement after being together for very long periods of time, and the very bottom has dropped out of their lives. There are those who have had painful experiences of divorce and they feel that their lives have become disoriented and damaged as a result.

Some see very few people anyway; they are tied up with work that prevents them from meeting other people with similar interests and outlooks; but there are also others who by their very make-up are quite happy at being on their own and their work brings them into contact with other people.

We are all unique but complex human beings. Our inner needs vary as much as our faces do but I also believe that we were made to give support to others, often people who are very different from ourselves who are lonely.

One of the things that is important about the teaching of Jesus is that he reminds us we need to take great care how we judge other people. In fact, we should never judge them, because the criterion by which we judge others brings us under judgement ourselves. Jesus himself made friends with all kinds of people in such a way that he was able to help many of them who were finding it difficult to sort out their lives.

We all fail in some way or another to show friendship to lonely people, and we have to take great care in our prayers and in our time of reflection that we notice those people who are in need of support in their loneliness.

In showing friendship and encouragement we may well be helping them to fulfil their role in life or even, may be, find a sense of direction for the first time.

July

'The one who sings prays twice'

About five years ago I was singing hymns in a worship service that I was leading and afterwards Val Machell, late co-leader of the Soundswell choir in Nottingham, came up to me and said, 'I want you to join our choir, and I'm not taking no for an answer.'

This invitation could not have come at a better time. It was in the early months of my bereavement, and I soon found that I was getting a great deal of satisfaction singing music from all over the world. I still enjoy singing hymns of course. This was a breath of fresh air, and during the holiday seasons of the year I find myself missing the uplift of regular singing and learning how to use my voice in a better way.

Singing can help through all kinds of life experiences, helping us to express our inner feelings better, or taking us away from negative thoughts. It can be likened to a form of praying. There is the famous saying attributed to St. Augustine that 'the one who sings prays twice!'

Singing offers a challenge to us. Perhaps people don't sing so much in their individual everyday activities. Let's find more delight in it. A good community choir, whether we read music or not is a great source of inspiration and in recent years there has been a healthy increase.

September

If you have a kindness shown...

(One reader suggested that the heading for this letter ought to be 'A good example of recycling.')

Nine years ago, I had to give up cycling because of surgery. I was very fond of my cycle because it had been given to me as a present when I worked in the Shetland Islands by my Lerwick congregation some 30 years ago. My previous cycle had been badly corroded by the sea salt!

My new cycle was a mountain bike. Not only did it serve me well in Shetland but also in St Albans and here in Nottingham for about 15 years-a first class way of getting some exercise, often meeting people in the streets and having a word with them. A very valuable part of community pastoral care.

Now it was lying in the garage. I was wondering whether to sell it on eBay, but then I had a thought. Although it needed cleaning and minor adjustments it was still in good working order, so I approached the headmaster of the local special needs school to see whether any students there could make good use of it. He immediately had in mind a candidate who would be given some training in cycle maintenance, and then given the cycle after he had finished renovating it.

Quite frankly I felt delighted that it could go to a 'good home.'

Somehow, I felt that the kind gesture of the Shetland folk presenting me with a cycle was being passed on to someone of a younger generation who would now make good use of it.

There used to be an old song which went, 'If you have a kindness shown, pass it on.'

Life must be full all kinds of good things that we can pass on. May we all join in the 'succession' of kind and generous acts as well as kind thoughts to others.

October

Breaking New Ground

This month, I'm breaking new ground. I'm making progress in writing a book. The idea has been simmering for a long time. There has been an element of procrastination and nervousness on my part, but several friends have expressed the view, unprompted by me, that I ought to write a book which would an anthology based on thoughts expressed in my monthly newsletter log.

It will require much concentrated work to prepare, and my hope is that it will be ready in the New Year when, 'God willing', I celebrate during the summer the 60th year or my ordination. The title will probably be 'In Times of Transition'.

It will cover a whole range of reflections on life both from the point of view of one's own involvement in dementia care homes, police chaplaincy, and general pastoral visiting, but also observations on living in times of great change, including personal change, especially over the last nine years. Hopefully, readers will find thoughts about ways in which we can be more proactively involved in society, in the environment, and in discovering insights which help our spiritual needs from whatever direction we come.

Many friends and relations have already offered help and advice which has been thankfully received. Your prayers would be valued in the undertaking of this venture.

With every blessing for the autumn season!

Look out for the green lights. Then go!

My holiday this year was a four-day visit via Eurostar to Paris. We made good use of tourist buses that gave excellent commentaries on their tours around the city from which we learnt a great deal about Paris and its attractions. Like many tourists, we were keen to see progress that is being made on Notre Dame.

The traffic, like any city, was intense. Not only roads full of buses, heavy vehicles and cars, but many different kinds and shapes of motorcycles, cycles, scooters, and even a few rickshaws. We had to take great care crossing roads, especially waiting for the green light to show.

When crossing lights are on red, we need to remember they are not just there to let the heavier traffic through, but to protect us when we are crossing; when they change, it's as if the 'green man' is saying, 'Now you can proceed; now you can cross.'

This can say something about life's journey. Are we responding to the right signals to direct our lives or are we so wrapped up in ourselves that we fail to see opportunities to go forward?

May we make our responses both great and small and respond to green light opportunities. We might need to consult others to find out what is the best way to go forward and, when the opportunity comes, take it!

Look out for the green lights. Then go!

December

Travelling 'contactless'

An advert on the back of a Nottingham bus said, 'travel contactless'. I quickly realised it meant that if you travel with the right 'app' on your smart phone and swipe it near the travel card censor on the bus your fare is then paid.

My mind, however, quickly went in a very different direction. In life we are all travelling on a journey, and on that journey none of us can travel 'contactless'. We need the contact, the support of other people.

We are living at a time when many have less and less close contact with other people in their daily affairs. Digitalisation has been a great boon to communications, but it means less contact is actually made directly with other human beings. People drive past our houses. A few might wave to us because they know us by sight Families do not live close to each other. Often if we want to make a transaction by computer or phone there may be a choice of up to 10 letters or numbers that have to be pressed. Even then we cannot be guaranteed an answer by a real person. Those living on their own especially can find themselves without support in their times of need.

'No man (or woman) is an island', John Donne reminds us, and there is also a spiritual dimension to this as well.

An important part of the Christian message for instance, is that with the coming of Jesus into the world we are celebrating a unique way in which God himself enters into human affairs When He comes, He is to be known by the name 'Emmanuel', meaning 'God with us'; in other words 'God in contact' with us, strengthening us through his coming, in our journeys through life.

My hope is that we will all find on our journey, a faith that will help us, keep us in touch, and guide us – through our friendships, through the help of good people of all kinds, and through to that source of strength which is 'beyond' ourselves.

With all good wishes for a very blessed Christmas and a Happy New Year.

Epilogue

On leaving school at 16, I trained as a public health inspector, nowadays called environmental health officers. I enjoyed this work. We were very involved in an extensive slum clearance undertaking in my home town of Dudley in the West Midlands. The area to be demolished was known as 'Flood Street' where small 'jerry' built terraced properties were constructed in the 19th century to house people working in the heavy industries of the Black Country. These homes had no bathrooms or gardens and often shared an outside toilet with several neighbours.

I have always believed that environmental well-being is important, but I was beginning to feel there was an even greater need for people to discover a faith to live by and I ought to offer to serve in the ordained ministry in the church. Three years elapsed before I could begin my vocational training. First there was National Service, followed by a year's work in a factory which manufactured tubular steel chairs. Both experiences were extremely valuable, living and working amongst people of many different backgrounds. The following six years were spent in preparing for ministry, for four years in Didsbury College, Bristol.

In this, the 60th anniversary year of my ordination, ministerial vocation still has a very important place in my life. I marvel at the way in which Pauline always gave me loving, caring, and wholehearted support. Likewise, my family also shared in this partnership. I would like to say a big 'thank you' to Simon, Anna and Elizabeth and their families for all their support. In their different ways they continue to help in spite of the fact that we are now so scattered.

Whilst preparing to give thanks for a long ministry I realise how much I have learnt about life through this call. It has not been easy; we all need forgiveness for our mistakes but in contrast there are so many experiences I treasure deeply.

Ministry is aided by many forms of prayer, Holy Scripture, theology, church history, lifelong learning and a great variety of people, including many who have been in my pastoral care. It also includes learning from those of other outlooks and religions. There is no end to the ways in which the Holy Spirit is able to guide us into new areas of activity.

This epilogue was intended to be a summing up of sixty years but, as the opening chapter of this anthology reminds us, 'life is full of the unexpected.' There is always a task for us to complete even when we have reached what might be described, biblically, as the 'twelfth hour' as a 'labourer in the vineyard.'

Unexpectedly the Covid-19 pandemic is creating fear and chaos in the world. A new phase is beginning, requiring the radical reorganisation of our lifestyles in order to help ourselves and others to find a meaningful way forward. Strangely enough, I feel that issues raised by the pandemic were, in essence, coming to light when these letters were first written. Now, many of their themes are more important than ever!

During an earlier part of my ministry in Lincoln, a situation arose where our main church was going through extremely difficult and divisive times. We decided we ought to have a time during the day when we remembered anyone who needed our prayers, and also prayed for many concerns causing distress in the world. We decided to have this prayer time as near as possible to midday.

This corporate prayer time started around 45 years ago, and has continued in the same simple form ever since. During the last few years 'Prayers @ 12' for me has frequently been spent in the summer-house at the top of the garden. This 'Summer-house Prayer Sanctuary' serves as a place where I can go especially at a time while churches and other places of worship are often closed because of the pandemic. Several friends join me in remembering prayers at twelve wherever they are. However we pray, many, especially those who have lost loved ones during the pandemic, are going to need our prayerful support for a very long time.

In times of transition, I have tried to serve faithfully in the name of Jesus to the best of my ability, travelling with Him along His way. This journeying still fills me with wonder and a continuing sense of exploration which eventually I believe, takes us beyond this life into The Eternal.

'Changed from glory into glory, till in heaven we take our place......Lost in wonder, love and praise.' (Charles Wesley)

Summing everything up, St Paul says, 'Fill your minds with those things that are good and that deserve praise, things that are true, noble, right, pure, lovely and honourable .... And the God of peace will be with you.' (Philippians: 4,8)

Cherry Tree in Woodthorpe Park early on Easter Sunday 2020

Acknowledgements

This anthology is a tribute to so many people who live out their lives unobtrusively serving others. It includes family, friends, many friends in policing, fellow worshippers and colleagues, teachers, neighbours, doctors, nurses, medical staff at every level and all who work to care for us, those who counsel the bereaved, and those who have recently opened new doors of service, especially in dementia care homes. How thankful we all are to all who have helped us in any way during this pandemic time of Covid-19.

Profits from the sale of this book will go into a 60th Ordination Anniversary year THANK OFFERING Fund, and will be used to help cancer and dementia research, and special needs of children.

Thank you to everyone who has helped in the compilation of this book:

- to the contributors of photographs: Revd. Dr. Andrew Fox of the Shetland district of the Methodist church, Jennifer Boateng for artwork, the Police Band and Nottinghamshire Police, and Margaret Brooks and Ian for organising the TocH lamp photograph;

- my daughter Anna and husband Jeff for designing and creating the cover for this book;

- to Bookprintingonline of Syston, Leicestershire for their guidance and help in preparing this book for publication;

- to the team of helpers, Jan Davies, Revd. John Hudson, Josephine McElroy, Malcolm Noble, Alan Sharp, and to Margaret Birch for the meticulous detailed help she has given with her editorial oversight and care.